Faster, Higher, Stro...

Welcome to the weird and wonderful world of experimental trains...

The Olympic motto 'Faster, Higher, Stronger' could just as easily be applied to the development of railways over the last two centuries. What follows is the story (so far) of our constant search for machines that will run faster, carry more people or freight more efficiently and reach places denied to existing technology.

Many of these machines were initially top-secret, hidden from sight to prevent rival nations or competitors from stealing the advantage, while others were famously high-profile, both in success and failure.

Some have gone on to change the way we travel and move goods, many others proved to be technological dead-ends, while some continue to be under development after several decades, waiting for technology and materials to catch up with the idea.

From high-pressure steam to magnetic levitation via rocket-propelled railcars and atomic locomotives, there's never been a shortage of creative engineers and inventors looking to change the world with new concepts. That's what makes this subject so fascinating – whether those ideas were utterly practical or verging on the insane, there have almost always been people willing to back them and develop prototypes to test the concept. We couldn't feature every experimental locomotive or train, but we've done our best to bring you a representative selection of the most successful, most radical and, of course, those that didn't fare so well.

In the beginning, all locomotives were experimental. After years of experiments with different forms of rail traction, the legendary Rainhill Trials of 1829 proved the superiority of Stephenson's design and, with gradual improvement, it remained dominant until the mid-20th century. However, before the end of the 19th century, electricity was showing that more efficient forms of propulsion were possible, and the advent of the internal combustion engine changed the world from the 1920s onwards.

In recent decades, the emphasis has been on achieving higher and higher speeds, with some predicting that steel wheels on steel rails have reached their limit. Concepts such as MAGLEV, and more recently, Hyperloop promise incredible speeds but have yet to deliver in the real world. Who knows what might come next? What we do know is that the human race will continue to try and go faster, move greater tonnages of freight and move around more efficiently, and that railways are likely to play a major part in that for the foreseeable future.

Ben Jones
Editor

CONTENTS

AUTHOR: Ben Jones

PRODUCTION EDITOR: Pauline Hawkins

DESIGN: Lucy Carnell, atg-media.com

COVER DESIGN: Mike Baumber

ADVERTISING MANAGER: Sue Keily

SALES EXECUTIVE: Craig Amess

REPROGRAPHICS: Paul Fincham, Jonathan Schofield and Angie Sisestean

PUBLISHER: Steve O'Hara

PUBLISHING DIRECTOR: Dan Savage

COMMERCIAL DIRECTOR: Nigel Hole

MARKETING MANAGER: Charlotte Park

DISTRIBUTION:
tradesales@mortons.co.uk
classicmagazines.co.uk/tradesales

PRINTED BY: William Gibbons And Sons, Wolverhampton

ISBN: 978-1-911276-48-7

PUBLISHED BY:
Mortons Media Group Ltd, Media Centre, Morton Way, Horncastle, Lincolnshire
LN9 6JR
Tel: 01507 529529

BULLEID'S 'LEADER'

One of the most controversial and most expensive failures of the steam era was O.V.S. Bulleid's unconventional 'Leader' 0-6-6-0T, designed to replace a range of vintage pre-Grouping classes on branch line and secondary work away from the Southern's electrified network. Just one of these massive machines was ever completed before the project was scrapped by BR. See page 45 for more. COLOUR-RAIL

English Electric's Gas Turbine 3 (GT3) was first proposed in the early-1950s but not built until a decade later, by which time BR was firmly committed to diesel traction. In main line tests, the red-brown prototype proved to be hugely powerful and capable, but like all railway gas turbines heavy fuel consumption was its downfall. Some argue that it should never have been built at all. RAILWAY MAGAZINE ARCHIVE

Designed to tilt around curves without losing speed, like a motorcyclist, the Advanced Passenger Train (APT) was BR's solution to increasing speeds on conventional routes such as the West Coast Main Line. It was built in both gas turbine and electric versions, although only the latter ever carried passengers. Drawing in influences from aerospace technology it was years ahead of its time but was sadly cancelled in the mid-1980s and most of the cars were scrapped. Today's Virgin West Coast 'Pendolino' tilting trains employ Italian technology imported from FIAT/Alstom. RAIL PHOTOPRINTS

Monorails have been around since the 19th century, but are still regarded as a futuristic rival to conventional modes of transport. However, they have so far failed to take-off as a realistic alternative to standard railways, except in very specific conditions. Duesseldorf Airport's 'H-Bahn' is a driverless suspended railway developed by Siemens and known as the 'SkyTrain'. ROBERT HUMM COLLECTION

A working replica of Stockton & Darlington Railway *Locomotion No. 1*, which hauled the world's first public train on September 27, 1825. ANDREW JEFFERY

Early Experiments in Steam

In less than 30 years at the beginning of the 19th century, steam engine technology went from stationary mining machines to powering the world's first inter-city railway

In the beginning, all railway locomotives were experimental. Railways and the vehicles that worked on them were developed over decades of trial and error, with ideas ranging from, quite literally, world-changing to the downright dangerous.

While railways worked by horses are thought to have been around in the north-east of England since the mid-17th century, they were traditionally limited to the load that could be pulled by a horse.

French inventor Nicolas-Joseph Cugnot was the first to develop a self-propelled, mechanical land vehicle in 1769. Significantly he was the first to employ a device for turning the reciprocating motion of a steam piston into rotary motion to turn the wheels of his machine. While the machine was said to be unstable, dangerous and slow, it laid the foundations for other inventors and engineers to develop self-propelled steam vehicles.

Most famous of these was Cornishman Richard Trevithick. As the son of a mining engineer, he was familiar with stationary steam engines from an early age and took a great interest in the development of high-pressure steam in the late-18th century. HP steam allowed the use of smaller cylinders to generate power, saving space and weight and Trevithick believed that engines could be made small enough to carry their own weight and tow a trailing load.

In 1801 he built the 'Puffing Devil', a self-propelled steam road locomotive which successfully carried six passengers from Camborne to Beacon – the first recognised instance of steam transport. Trevithick's first rail locomotive was built by the Coalbrookdale company in Shropshire around 1803, although it is not known whether it ever ran.

The design incorporated a single horizontal cylinder enclosed in a return-flue boiler. A flywheel drove the wheels on one side through spur gears and the axles were mounted directly on the boiler. In 1802 it was followed by a high-pressure

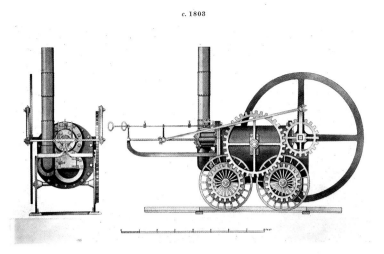

c. 1803

ABOVE: A sketch of Richard Trevithick's Coalbrookdale locomotive, thought to have been built around 1803. SCIENCE MUSEUM

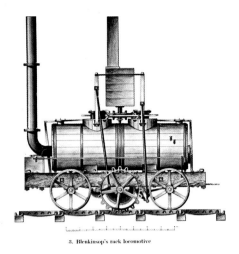

3. Blenkinsop's rack locomotive

ABOVE: John Blenkinsop's rack locomotive of 1812, as used on the Middleton Railway in Leeds. SCIENCE MUSEUM

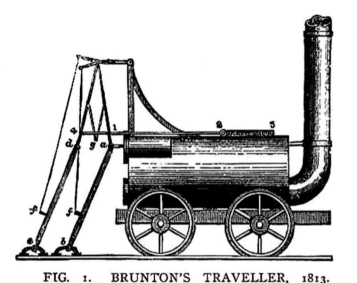

FIG. 1. BRUNTON'S TRAVELLER, 1813.

ABOVE: Brunton's 'Steam Horse' showing the unusual legs which pushed the locomotive along the rails and allowed it to climb steep gradients. WIKIMEDIA COMMONS

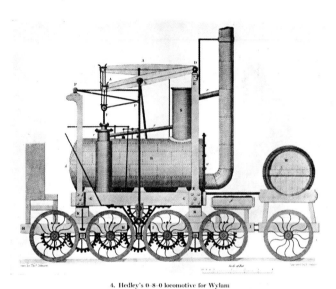

4. Hedley's 0-8-0 locomotive for Wylam

ABOVE: Hedley's geared locomotive for Wylam Colliery in its eight-wheel form, after rebuilding to spread the weight and reduce damage to brittle iron rails. SCIENCE MUSEUM

steam engine built to power a hammer at the Pen-y-Darren Ironworks in Merthyr Tydfil, South Wales. With assistance from Rees Jones and Samuel Homfray, the works' owner, the engine was mounted on wheels and transformed into a railway locomotive.

To win a 500 guinea bet with a rival ironmaster, Homfray said that the locomotive would be able to haul ten tons of iron over almost ten miles of the Merthyr Tydfil tramroad from Penydarren to Abercynon. On February 21, 1804 it did just that, hauling ten tons of iron, five wagons and 70 men over the distance in just over four hours at an average speed of 2.4mph. Despite some of the cast iron plates of the tramroad breaking under the weight of Trevithick's locomotive, it proved the principle that a steam locomotive could haul more than its own weight over gentle gradients using a smooth iron road.

Over the next few years, he designed and demonstrated more railway locomotives, including the Newcastle locomotive of 1804 and the famous 'Catch Me Who Can', which ran on a circular demonstration track close to the current Euston Square underground station in London. However,

public response to the 'steam circus' was disappointing and marked the end of Trevithick's railway locomotive development.

It was not until 1812 that further developments were made, when Matthew Murray built the world's first commercially viable steam locomotive. An innovative designer born in Newcastle in 1765, Murray worked in many fields, including designing machine tools and improved machinery for the textile industry.

Salamanca built on Trevithick's high-pressure steam, but employed two cylinders rather than one to give a smoother, more even delivery of power. It was supplied to John Blenkinsop, the manager of Brandling's Middleton Colliery on the outskirts of Leeds. In 1811, Blenkinsop had patented a system using a toothed wheel and rack to allow lightweight steam locomotives to pull at least 20 times their own weight. The toothed wheel was driven by connecting rods and meshed with a toothed rail on one side of the track. *Salamanca* was so successful that it was joined by three more locomotives, *Lord Wellington*, *Prince Regent* and *Marquis Wellington*. Steam operation continued until

1835 when the ageing and increasingly unreliable engines were replaced by horses – two locomotives exploded killing their drivers, but the Middleton Railway remains open today – the world's oldest continuously operational railway.

Around the same time as Murray's experiments Christopher Blackett, owner of Wylam Colliery near Newcastle, was conducting his own trials using adhesion-only steam locomotives. The result was *Puffing Billy*, constructed in 1813/14 by William Hedley, Jonathan Forster and Timothy Hackworth. It was the first commercial adhesion steam locomotive and, with two similar machines, hauled chaldron wagons loaded with coal from Wylam pit to the docks at Lemington-on-Tyne until 1862.

Puffing Billy incorporated a number of novel features, patented by Hedley, which were to prove important to the development of locomotives. It had two vertical cylinders on either side of the boiler, and partly enclosed by it, and drove a crankshaft beneath the frames, from which gears drove and also coupled the wheels allowing better traction.

▶

ABOVE: The original *Locomotion* of 1825, on display at the Head of Steam Museum in Darlington along with several other early locomotives. BEN JONES

immediately improved the haulage of the coal from the mine using fixed engines. However, he had taken an interest in Blenkinsop and Blackett's engines and persuaded colliery managers to fund a 'travelling engine'. He confirmed Blackett's observation that the friction of the wheels was sufficient on an iron railway without cogs but still used a cogwheel system in transmitting power to the wheels.

Blücher was built by George Stephenson in 1814; the first of a series of locomotives that established his reputation as a designer and laid the foundations for his pivotal role in the development of the railways. *Blücher* could pull a train of 30 tons at 4mph up a gradient of 1-in-450. A second machine with various improvements was built in 1815.

In 1816, in response to poor track causing frequent derailments, Stephenson devised a new rail chair and used half-lap joints between the rails instead of butt-joints. Wrought iron replaced cast iron wheels and he used the steam pressure of the boiler to provide 'steam spring' suspension. Engines constructed on these principles from 1816 were being used until 1841 as locomotives and until 1856 as stationary engines.

The *Killingworth Billy* or *Billy* was built in 1826 to Stephenson's design by Robert Stephenson & Co. It ran on the Killingworth Railway until 1881, when it was presented to the City of Newcastle. It is currently preserved at the Stephenson Railway Museum.

Steam Elephant was a six-wheeled locomotive built in 1815 for the Wallsend Waggonway, an 'edge railway' built to Stephenson's favoured 4ft 8in gauge.

It also had a centre-flue boiler with two vertical cylinders of about 9in by 24in set into its top centreline. The cylinders drove slide bar mounted beams which turned crankshafts driving the axles through 2:1 reduction gears between the frames. It weighed about 7.5 tons and had a top speed of around 4.5mph and could haul around 90 tons over short distances.

Stockton & Darlington

By the early-1820s, the potential of steam locomotives working over iron rails was becoming obvious and in 1825 the world's first public railway to employ them opened for business. The Stockton & Darlington Railway (S&DR) opened on September 27, 1825 and connected collieries around Shildon with Stockton and Darlington. The rapid movement of coal was a lucrative business, and the line was extended to Middlesbrough, further down the River Tees. Coal waggons were hauled by steam locomotives from 1825, but passenger coaches drawn by horses until 1833.

The S&DR's first locomotive was *Locomotion No. 1* (originally named *Active*), incorporating the many improvements pioneered by George Stephenson on his Killingworth locomotives. It used high-pressure steam from a centre-flue boiler, with a steam blast in the chimney to drive

However, at eight tons it was too heavy for the cast iron waggonway plates and broke them, giving encouragement to the opponents of steam traction at the time. It was redesigned with four axles to spread the weight more evenly, but eventually rebuilt with four driving wheels when improved track was introduced around 1830. Maximum speed was around 5mph.

Another development of 1813 was William Brunton's Steam Horse, constructed by the Butterley Ironworks in Derbyshire. Uniquely, it employed a pair of mechanical legs which gripped the rails at the rear of the engine and pushed it along the rails at a maximum of 3mph. Also known as the 'Mechanical Traveller', the contraption was built to work between Butterley's limestone quarry at Crich and the Cromford Canal, a line with a 1-in-50 gradient which was generally regarded as unsuitable for adhesion working at the time. A second locomotive with a large

boiler was built for Newbottle Colliery in Co. Durham and worked over a 1-in-36 gradient, but its boiler exploded in 1815, killing 13 spectators during a demonstration. The cause of the world's first recorded railway disaster was the locomotive's safety valves being screwed down too tight, and therefore not able to release the excess pressure in the boiler.

Stronger Rails

From around 1819, the introduction of stronger, malleable iron rails in place of wrought iron allowed heavier adhesion locomotives to operate without the need for rack assistance.

Between 1814 and 1826, George Stephenson built a number of experimental steam locomotives for Killingworth Colliery in the north-east of England. Stephenson had been appointed as engine-wright at Killingworth in 1812 and

9. Braithwaite and Ericsson's 0-2-2 *Novelty* well-tank locomotive

ABOVE: Braithwaite & Ericsson's *Novelty*, one of the five locomotives that participated in the Rainhill Trials of October 1829 and the closest challenger to Stephenson's *Rocket*. SCIENCE MUSEUM

two vertical cylinders enclosed within the boiler. A pair of yokes above them transmitted the power downwards, through pairs of connecting rods. It was the first locomotive to have coupling rods linking its driving wheels, rather than chains or gears. It had a top speed of 15mph.

Locomotion became obsolete very quickly but was rebuilt and remained in service until 1841 when it became a stationary engine. Fortunately, this significant machine was preserved in 1857 and from 1892 until 1975 it was on display at Darlington Bank Top station.

The commercial success of the S&DR quickly led to the development of other railway schemes, the most famous of which linked the most important city of the Industrial Revolution, Manchester, with its gateway to the world – the port city of Liverpool. The development of the world's first inter-city railway, with huge potential for freight and passenger traffic, would clearly lead to lucrative orders for locomotives and all the major players of the time were keen to promote their machines as the best tool for the job.

Rainhill Trials

With construction of the L&MR heading towards completion, the railway's management organised a competition in October 1829 to find the best steam locomotive for the new railway. Five machines competed, running back and forth along a 1.75 mile length of level track at Rainhill in Lancashire. George and Robert Stephenson's *Rocket* was the only locomotive to complete the trials, and was declared the winner with George and Robert Stephenson given the contract to build locomotives for the railway.

Three notable figures from the early days of engineering were selected as judges: John Urpeth Rastrick, a locomotive engineer from Stourbridge, Nicholas Wood, a mining engineer

from Killingworth with considerable locomotive design experience and John Kennedy, a Manchester cotton spinner and a major supporter of the railway.

Locomotives were subjected to a variety of tests and conditions, including weighing, test runs totalling 35 miles over level track at an average of 'not less than 10mph' – quicker than the Stockton & Darlington's average speed of 8mph at the time. Once the first round of runs had been completed, equivalent to a run from Liverpool to Manchester, it could be coaled, watered and serviced ready for a second batch of runs equivalent to the return run to Liverpool.

Although ten locomotives were entered, only five actually made it as far as starting the trials; *Cycloped*, built by Thomas Shaw Brandreth; John Ericsson and John Braithwaite's *Novelty*; Timothy Burstall's *Perseverance*; *Sans Pareil* by Timothy Hackworth and *Rocket*.

Cycloped was the first to drop out;

it employed a horse walking on a drive belt for power, and was withdrawn after an accident caused the horse to burst through the floor of the engine.

Perseverance was damaged in transit to Rainhill and spent five days under repair before it could run. It failed to reach the required 10mph on its first tests and was withdrawn from the trial.

Hackworth's *Sans Pareil* nearly completed the trials, though at first there was some doubt as to whether it would be allowed to compete as it was 300lb overweight. It completed eight trips before cracking a cylinder. Despite the failure it was purchased by the L&MR and ran for two years before moving to the Bolton & Leigh Railway.

Last to drop out was *Novelty*. It was an advanced machine for 1829; lighter and faster than the other locomotives in the competition and became the crowd favourite. Reaching an astonishing 28mph on the first day of competition, it later suffered a failure which could not be fixed properly on site and failed again the next day, the damage forcing it out of the competition.

Rocket averaged 12mph, achieving a top speed of 30mph and scooped the £500 prize as well as a contract to produce locomotives for the Liverpool & Manchester Railway.

The Stephensonian model went on to become the dominant arrangement for steam locomotives across the world, gradually evolving to become larger, more efficient and more powerful throughout the 19th century and well into the 20th.

Many engineers and inventors proposed alternatives to Stephenson's design, but none had the enormous worldwide impact of those locomotives designed and developed in the collieries of north-east England. As we'll see over the coming pages, locomotive engineers went to great lengths to design better, faster and more efficient locomotives after 1829, some to good effect and others much less so! ●

STEPHENSON'S "ROCKET" Built 1829
THE ORIGINAL IS NOW IN SOUTH KENSINGTON MUSEUM

ABOVE: Rocket – the winner of the 1829 Liverpool & Manchester Railway trials and the machine that set the template for more than a century of steam locomotive development RAILWAY MAGAZINE ARCHIVE

ABOVE: North Pacific Coast Railroad 3ft gauge 4-4-0 No. 21 *Thomas-Stetson* is thought to have been one of the first 'cab forwards'. It was rebuilt from NPCRR No. 5 at Sausalito Works in 1901 and scrapped in 1905. ROBERT HUMM COLLECTION

Back-to-Front Engines

Historically, steam locomotive crews had a restricted view of the road ahead from the footplate. This problem got worse as locomotives grew larger and more powerful and so engineers in Europe and North America devised 'cab forward' designs to give drivers the same clear view enjoyed by diesel and electric crews.

ABOVE: Italy's Rete Adriatica railway was the first to introduce a 'cab forward' steam locomotive – a four-cylinder Plancher compound 4-6-0 of 1900. It was the first of several designs tested in Italy. No. 5031 was the last of the second series, built by Ernesto Breda in 1905. Although the complex Plancher system had its flaws, a total of 43 locomotives were built by Breda and Borsig up to 1906 and one was tested in France. ROBERT HUMM COLLECTION

ABOVE: In 1936, one of the former RA locomotives, by now Italian State Railways (FS) Class 670, was rebuilt with an experimental Franco-Crosti boiler, fitted with a streamlined casing and renumbered 672.001. On test it showed a 22% saving in fuel compared to its superheated Class 671 sisters but was scrapped by the end of the decade as FS focused on electrification of its network. The unusual machine leaves Milano Centrale with an express. ROBERT HUMM COLLECTION

ABOVE: Breda catalogue showing the Rete Adriatica four-cylinder compound 4-6-0. ROBERT HUMM COLLECTION

ABOVE: Royal Prussian Railways (KPEV) also investigated 'cab forward' designs with two 4-4-4 express locomotives designed by Kuhn and built by Henschel & Sohn in 1904. No. 561 (pictured) was a three-cylinder compound with one cab ahead of a boiler in the conventional direction. Most of the controls were in the cab and the driver communicated with his fireman via a speaking tube! After being exhibited in the USA in 1904 it was rebuilt as a standard 4-4-4 in 1912. ROBERT HUMM COLLECTION

ABOVE: Before the Second World War, Germany's Deutsche Reichsbahn tested various experimental steam locomotives, including the streamlined 'cab forward' 4-6-4 No. 05 003 of 1937, which used pulverised coal as fuel. It was rebuilt as a conventional 4-6-4 in 1944, and again by Deutsche Bundesbahn in 1950. ROBERT HUMM COLLECTION

ABOVE: The Southern Pacific Railroad in the USA was the best-known user of 'cab forward' locomotives, buying a series of progressively larger and more powerful classes (AC-1 to AC-12) from Baldwin between 1909 and 1944. The concept was particularly suited to the SP's long routes through the Sierra Nevada mountains in California, which had miles of tunnels and snow sheds that created dangerous conditions for loco crews. All the SP's 'cab forwards' were oil-burners. 'AC-10' No. X4211 was built by Baldwin in 1941. ROBERT HUMM COLLECTION

ABOVE: The USSR 'Stalinets' TP1-1 2-10-2 of 1939/40 was an anthracite-gas-diesel hybrid with eight opposed pistons that proved to be a technical failure and an engineering nightmare. It performed no useful work for Soviet Railways. It ran just 1,790km at the Shcherbinka test track near Moscow and only worked properly at speeds below 30kph. ROBERT HUMM COLLECTION ●

ABOVE: The Southern Railway's 'King Arthur' 4-6-0s were subject to several experimental forms of smoke deflector and blastpipe modifications to cure drifting smoke issues. No. 772 *Sir Percivale* received these large deflectors in the 1930s. The class was later fitted with smaller deflectors as standard. RAIL PHOTOPRINTS

A Clearer View

Many classes of steam locomotive experienced problems with exhaust smoke obscuring the view ahead for crews – creating dangerous situations where signals and obstructions could be missed. Here are just a few of the modifications made to try and solve the problem.

ABOVE: An earlier 'King Arthur' smoke deflector trial was this scoop fitted behind the chimney of Eastleigh-built 'N15' No. 450 *Sir Kay*, soon after it was delivered in June 1925. RAILWAY MAGAZINE ARCHIVE

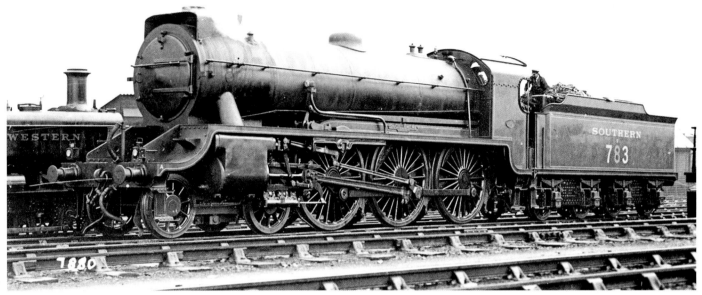

ABOVE: Many of the smoke deflector trials did little to improve the aesthetics of their subjects. 'Scotch Arthur' No. 783 *Sir Gillemere* was built by North British in 1925 and later fitted with an air scoop ahead of the chimney in an unsuccessful attempt to cure drifting smoke. RAILWAY MAGAZINE ARCHIVE

ABOVE: Another class that suffered with drifting smoke was the LMS 'Royal Scot' 4-6-0. This 1932 modification to No. 6161 *King's Own* radically altered the appearance of the locomotive by adding a deflector cone to the smokebox door, modified smokebox barrel and smaller stovepipe chimney. More conventional side-mounted deflectors were later fitted to the whole class. RAIL PHOTOPRINTS

ABOVE: When the 'A3s' received Kylchap double blastpipes and chimneys in 1958-60, the softer exhaust created visibility problems. No. 60061 *Pretty Polly* (seen here at King's Cross Top Shed on March 23, 1961) was unsuccessfully tested with small winglets either side of the chimney. At the suggestion of King's Cross shedmaster Peter Townend, German-style Witte smoke deflectors were fitted to 57 of the class from 1961 onwards and proved to be extremely effective. RAIL PHOTOPRINTS

ABOVE: LNER double-chimney 'A3' No. 60097 *Humorist* was the subject of various smoke clearing trials before and after Nationalisation and finally received side-mounted deflectors similar to those on the Peppercorn 'A1s' and 'A2s'. On May 26, 1956, the 'A3' passes Jamestown on the approach to the Forth Bridge. RAIL PHOTOPRINTS ●

The Midland's Mysterious Paget Locomotive

ABOVE: The only known photograph of No. 2299, an official Midland Railway works portrait. RAILWAY MAGAZINE ARCHIVE

Known as the 'Paget Locomotive', or 'Paget's Folly' by its critics, 2-6-2 No. 2299 was an experimental steam locomotive constructed at Derby Works in 1907/08 to the design of MR General Superintendent, Sir Cecil Paget. His novel concept, with many ingenious features could have played a greater role in shaping the future of steam locomotives, but internal politics at Derby Works reduced it to little more than a footnote in British railway history.

In 1906 Paget, son of MR chairman Sir George Ernest Paget and Derby Works manager, had been widely tipped to replace Samuel Johnson as Locomotive Superintendent but the job instead went to Richard Deeley. Cecil Paget remained as his assistant until 1907 when he was promoted to become the company's first General Superintendent, responsible for train operations and the men associated with it. Deeley, reluctantly, had his title changed to Chief Mechanical Engineer and was unhappy at losing influence over the operational side of his locomotive fleet. The resulting tensions within the MR did Paget's project no favours at Derby Works.

The MR shrouded the locomotive in secrecy, with the result that there is only one known photograph, only released after the Grouping of 1923, which created the 'Big Four' companies and saw the MR become part of the new London Midland & Scottish Railway. By that time the locomotive had been scrapped for almost a decade.

Inspired by the Willans stationary engine concept, which was being used with great success in electricity generating stations of the time, the locomotive had no fewer than eight single-acting cylinders arranged in two groups of four placed between the first and second and second and third driving axles. Rotary steam distribution valves were placed over each and a bronze sleeve in the valve body was rotated to control piston cut-off. Two were connected to the leading driving axle of the 2-6-2. Four were connected – two each side – to the middle axle with the final two situated behind the rearmost driving axle. These drove a jackshaft which operated and reversed the valves, and cut-off was controlled by rotary sleeves.

The large diameter boiler had an unusual integral steel firebox, lined with firebricks, as used in industrial furnaces. This eliminated the need for an expensive copper firebox, as was standard for British steam locomotives,

and around 75% of the firebox stays.

The locomotive was also well ahead of its time in other details, including the view of the line ahead from the cab and ash disposal from the ashpan and smokebox – all of which were designed with crews and fitters in mind.

The frames were placed outside the driving wheels, crucially providing the space to accommodate the four large diameter cylinders in two overlapping barrels. Pony trucks were fitted front and rear, making it the first 2-6-2 tender locomotive in the UK and the only example of this type until Sir Nigel Gresley's 'V2' 2-6-2 of 1936 for the LNER.

Paget initially financed the project himself, but ran out of money and the MR is said to have covered the shortfall on the understanding that all subsequent tests were undertaken on its terms.

Reports suggest No. 2299 was free-steaming and smooth at speeds of up to 80mph but it experienced problems with seizing of the phosphor bronze sleeves in the cast iron steam chest and leakage in the glands and piston rings. In 1912, one of the rotary valves seized while on a test run and it was reported that No. 2299 blocked a main line for seven hours. As a result it was put in store, sheeted

The "Paget" Locomotive

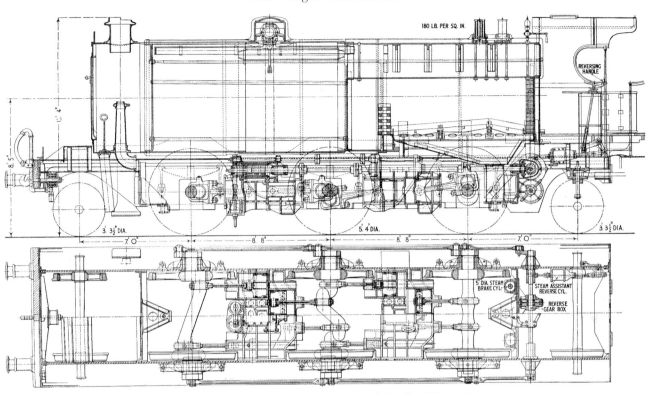

Fig. 3—General arrangement drawing and plan of the "Paget" locomotive

ABOVE: General Arrangement (GA) drawing of Paget's revolutionary locomotive. BEN JONES COLLECTION

over and hidden in a corner of the Derby Works paint shop until 1915 when it was broken up. At the time, Cecil Paget was away in France commanding the Royal Engineers Railway Operating Division.

Almost nothing was known of the locomotive until 1924 when author E.L. Ahrons mentioned it in his masterpiece *The British Steam Locomotive*. In 1945, the-then LMS Chief Mechanical Engineer Charles Fairburn broke the previous silence on No. 2299 by releasing works drawings to *The Railway Gazette*. The drawings were used alongside a detailed description by Paget's MR colleague James Clayton, who assisted with the design of the locomotive. At the time, Clayton had recently retired as Personal Assistant to Southern Railway CME O.V.S. Bulleid. Interestingly, Bulleid's ill-fated 'Leader' locomotives also used sleeve valves, the only other British steam locomotives to do so.

While on the surface Paget's heroic venture appeared to be a failure, its supporters were convinced that it could have changed the direction of British steam traction had its designer been allowed to continue. The rotary sleeve valves could have been modified for greater reliability or exchanged for piston valves given more time, but the cheap and simple boiler was years ahead of its time and the perfectly balanced, free-running design could have exerted a much greater influence on British locomotive design if it hadn't been the victim of internal jealousies and conservative thinking at Derby. ●

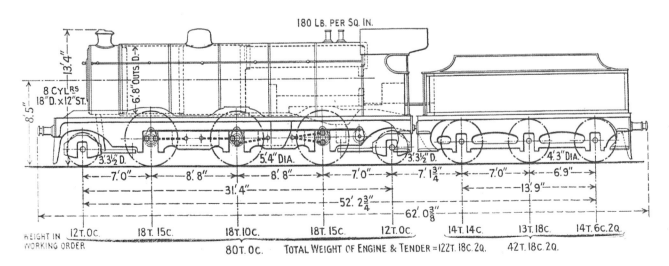

Fig. 2—Diagram of "Paget" locomotive showing principal dimensions and weights

ABOVE: Side elevation drawing of Paget's revolutionary locomotive. BEN JONES COLLECTION

Steam Turbines

Inspired by developments in shipbuilding, steam turbine propulsion was the subject of various locomotive experiments in the first half of the 20th century, promising greater power and efficiency over conventional steam traction.

ABOVE: Built by Beyer, Peacock of Manchester to a Swedish design, the Beyer-Ljungström steam turbine locomotive was tested on the Midland Main Line in 1926-28. Although it was more powerful than existing steam types, it did not deliver the expected savings in fuel to offset its higher construction and operating costs. ROBERT HUMM COLLECTION

The Reid-Ramsey Turbine-Electric

As far back as 1910, the advanced Reid-Ramsey Turbine-Electric was the first steam turbine locomotive built in the UK. Built by the North British Locomotive Company (NBL) to a design devised by the company's Deputy Chairman and Chief Managing Director Sir Hugh Reid, the machine featured a conventional superheated locomotive boiler feeding an impulse turbine running at 3,000rpm. This was coupled to a dynamo producing between 200V and 600V DC to power four 275hp axle-mounted traction motors. In modern terms it was a miniature coal-fired power station on

wheels, and considerably ahead of its time.

Theoretically, a steam turbine is much more efficient than a reciprocal steam engine but only when the turbine vents into a near vacuum, and when it is running at high speed. A large condenser positioned at the front of the locomotive created the near-vacuum while the high speeds were handled by an electrical transmission.

The turbine-generator assembly was housed in the central body section between the boiler and condenser. Both automatic vacuum and Westinghouse compressed air brakes were fitted, the latter

presumably for use with Caledonian Railway air-braked stock of the time.

An ejector type condenser, in which steam was condensed by direct contact with a spray of cold water, was used. Steam turbines do not require internal lubrication so the condensed water was oil-free and could be pumped back into the boiler. Water was handled by centrifugal pumps driven by auxiliary turbines.

According to reports of the time, circulating water was pumped from tanks either side of the boiler into the ejector condenser and mixed with water from the condensed exhaust steam. It then entered the hot well where a second pump fed it to cooling tubes at the front of the locomotive. From there it was returned to the water tanks.

Total weight was 132 tonnes, with just 89t available for adhesion; possibly a result of the 4-4-0+0-4-4 configuration chosen. Contemporary opinion (taken from *The Engineer* magazine) was that a steam-electric locomotive was too complicated and expensive.

Little is known about the locomotive and whether the concept was successful, but journals of the time report that it underwent preliminary main line tests on Caledonian and North British Railway lines in Scotland 'with a saloon carriage attached'. However, what is known is that by 1924 the Reid-Ramsey locomotive had been dismantled and rebuilt using two turbines, one powering each bogie via geared drives.

One of the major issues for turbine drive on railway locomotives is that they work most effectively at continuous high speeds, as in a power station. While this could have been appropriate for a long-distance express locomotive, the maximum power of around 1,000hp would have been insufficient for such duties, even in 1910. The turbine also wasted large quantities of water when starting up, and would have been unsuitable for trains stopping frequently or shunting work. Reverse-running performance is likely to have been poor, and the delicate turbines and other equipment were ill-suited to the vibration, rough track, and dirty environment of early-20th century steam railways. ●

LOCOMOTIVES OF 1910

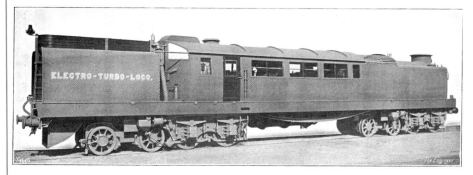

THE REID-RAMSAY ELECTRO-TURBO LOCOMOTIVE

ABOVE: A clipping from *The Engineer* magazine of January 1911 with a very rare photograph of the Reid-Ramsay 'Electro Turbo Loco' built in 1910. ROBERT HUMM COLLECTION

The Reid-MacLeod Turbine Locomotive

Very little is known about the North British Locomotive Company's Reid-MacLeod turbine locomotive. It was an early attempt at a steam turbine locomotive, rebuilt from the Reid-Ramsey steam turbine electric of 1910 (see above). For this machine, Hugh Reid, Deputy Chairman and Chief Managing Director of NBL was jointly credited with James MacLeod, a Glasgow turbine expert.

Electrical transmission would have been cutting edge technology in 1910, and it is thought to have been problematic because it was eliminated in the rebuild and replaced with a mechanical transmission. However, the frames, bogies, and boiler were re-used to produce a locomotive with a 4-4-0+0-4-4 wheel arrangement.

Some accounts describe two turbines per bogie – one for each direction of travel, while other reports describe a turbine consisting of three blade rings for high pressure steam forward, low pressure steam forward, and reverse. The high-pressure turbine was closest to the boiler to reduce heat losses and fed into the low pressure turbine, which in turn fed the adjacent condenser at the front of the locomotive. While the condenser would have worked well when running forwards, it would have been less useful when running in reverse as the cooling effect would have been much reduced.

The boiler and chimney were situated at the rear of the locomotive with the driving cab in the centre.

The rebuilt locomotive was displayed at the British Empire Exhibition at Wembley in 1924, although it may not have been complete at the time as trials did not start until two years later. Recorded trials ran on the LNER between Glasgow and Edinburgh in March 1926-April 1927. The first run, hauling just two coaches, failed at Greenhill after problems with the condenser pumps, but reports comment on an "almost entire absence of vibration, oscillation, and rail pounding". A second run is said to have suffered axlebox problems and a turbine failure. There's no confirmation of whether it ever ran again after 1927 and the machine remained dumped at the back of NBL's works in Glasgow until it was scrapped around 1940 to make room for air-raid shelters. ●

NORTH BRITISH LOCOMOTIVE COMPANY'S GEARED STEAM TURBINE CONDENSING LOCOMOTIVE

ABOVE: An official works portrait of the North British Locomotive Co.'s Reid-MacLeod steam-turbine prototype dating from the mid-1920s.
ABOVE RIGHT: NBL advert promoting the Reid-MacLeod locomotive taken from a contemporary issue of *The Railway Gazette*. ROBERT HUMM COLLECTION (2)

Beyer-Ljungström Turbine Locomotive

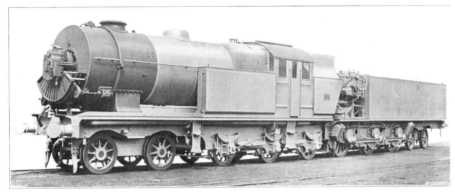

LJUNGSTROM TURBINE LOCOMOTIVE BEYER. PEACOCK

ABOVE: Official works portrait of the Beyer-Ljungström steam-turbine locomotive showing the large rotating pre-heater equipment protruding from the front of the smokebox. ROBERT HUMM COLLECTION

The 1920s saw a third steam-turbine locomotive tested on Britain's railways, in this case based on a Swedish design which achieved some success in its home country.

Swedish engineer Frederik Ljungström devised a condensing turbo locomotive formed of two coupled vehicles, one carrying the boiler and the other the condenser with the turbines sitting between the two and driving the leading three geared axles under the condenser. The other wheels, a bogie and three axles under the boiler section carried the weight of the equipment but were not powered, while the rearmost axle was powered for reverse working.

Built in 1921, it was 75ft long and weighed 126 tons. It was tested on the Swedish rail network, developing 1,800hp with the turbine running at 9,200 revolutions per minute (rpm) and capable of maintaining 60mph on level track with a train of 475 tons. However, the most eye-opening statistic was its thermal efficiency, which at a reported 14.7% was more than twice as efficient as a conventional steam locomotive.

Spotting its potential, British locomotive builder Beyer, Peacock of Manchester built a similar machine to Ljungström's patents in 1924. It underwent main line testing on the LMS Midland Division in 1926-28, including covering 5,400 miles over several months working on the Midland Main Line between St Pancras and Derby.

At 75mph, the turbine ran at 10,500rpm and produced an impressive maximum tractive effort of 40,320lb. Maximum design power was 2,000hp, although no more than 1,650hp was ever achieved in practice.

Even to modern eyes this was a strange looking machine with a similar wheel arrangement to the Swedish locomotive, including outside frames under the firebox end of the boiler, six 5ft 3in driving wheels grouped under the condenser section and bogies at each end for bi-directional working. Contained within the smokebox area beneath the chimney was a rotating media air pre-heater warmed by flue gases ejected from the firebox, while protruding from the front of the firebox was a drive unit for friction rollers that rotated the preheater. On top of the rear section, four large upward facing fans drew in air for the condenser.

Weighing in at almost 144 tons it proved to be a capable locomotive, capable of hauling heavier loads than the existing Midland 4-4-0s still being used by the LMS at the time. However, the promised savings in running costs did not materialise and so the extra cost of constructing the much more complicated design could not be justified by the LMS.

After 1928, the prototype was withdrawn and dismantled. Performance was reportedly hindered by leaks of air into the condenser, spoiling the necessary vacuum, but also by poor combustion. ●

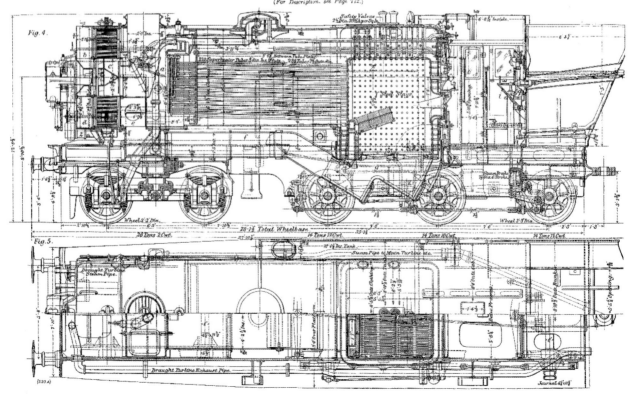

2,000-H.P. LJUNGSTRÖM TURBINE LOCOMOTIVE.

CONSTRUCTED BY MESSRS. BEYER, PEACOCK AND COMPANY, LIMITED, ENGINEERS, MANCHESTER.

(For Description, see Page 772.)

ABOVE: General Arrangement drawing of the Beyer-Ljungström locomotive. RAILWAY MAGAZINE ARCHIVE

Armstrong-Whitworth Turbine-Electric

Perhaps the least-known of the early steam turbine locomotives of the 1920s, was built by Armstrong-Whitworth and delivered to the Lancashire & Yorkshire Railway in 1922.

Designed by D.M. Ramsay, thought to be the same designer responsible for the earlier Reid-Ramsay prototype, the experimental machine was built by A-W at its Newcastle-upon-Tyne works. It featured a 2-6-0+0-6-2 wheel arrangement with the six coupled wheels on each section driven by a jackshaft coupled to two 275hp electric motors.

The front unit carried the boiler; beneath it was an Oerlikon compound turbine direct-coupled to a three-phase AC generator. The rear unit carried fuel, water, and the air-cooled rotary evaporative condenser. The Mirrlees-Watson condenser was fitted to create a sufficient exhaust vacuum for efficient turbine operation rather than to save water, but proved unable to do its job to good effect.

When delivered to the LYR at Horwich Works, the machine weighed a whopping 156 tons, 34t more than expected and with a prohibitive axleload of 24t. However, the company's civil engineer allowed it to venture as far as Bolton on April 5, 1922.

Unfortunately, performance was poor, water and fuel consumption were much higher than expected and design flaws led to poor fuel combustion and difficulty in maintaining the condenser vacuum.

Modifications were made, including a new chimney and condenser, which led to some improvement, but the machine was still far too heavy and performance was inferior to a standard LYR 2-4-2T on one test run!

Its last test runs took place in May 1923, after which it was returned to Armstrong-Whitworth and dismantled. ●

RAMSAY CONDENSING TURBO-ELECTRIC LOCOMOTIVE

SCIENTIFIC AMERICAN

[Entered at the Post Office of New York, N. Y., as Second Class Matter. Copyright, 1897, by Munn & Co.]

A WEEKLY JOURNAL OF PRACTICAL INFORMATION, ART, SCIENCE, MECHANICS, CHEMISTRY, AND MANUFACTURES

Vol. LXXVII.—No. 10.]
Established 1845.

NEW YORK, SEPTEMBER 4, 1897.

[$3.00 A YEAR.
WEEKLY.

ABOVE: The remarkable Armstrong-Whitworth/Ramsay steam turbine-electric of 1922. Overweight and underpowered, it did little useful work and was returned to A-W for dismantling in 1923. ROBERT HUMM COLLECTION

Fig. 4.—THE HEILMANN ELECTRIC LOCOMOTIVE.—[See page 152.]

LEFT: In the mid- to late-1890s, a series of three experimental steam-electric locomotives designed by Jacques Heilmann were built for the Chemins de Fer de l'Ouest in France. This clipping from the Scientific American newspaper of September 1897 shows No. 8001, one of the two larger prototypes built that year using engines built by Willans & Robinson of Rugby. Like other steam-turbines they were designed to eliminate the unbalanced 'hammer blow' forces of conventional steam locomotives. However, they can also be regarded as direct ancestors of the diesel-electric locomotives. ROBERT HUMM COLLECTION

Stanier's Turbomotive

LMS Chief Mechanical Engineer William Stanier earned his fame by designing some of the most successful and numerous British steam locomotive types, but he also experimented with steam turbine propulsion.

ABOVE: No. 46202 in 1949, after it had gained smoke deflectors to lift drifting smoke away from the cab and been repainted in BR mixed traffic lined black. The one-off prototype passes Halton Junction with a Liverpool-Euston express. RAIL PHOTOPRINTS

ABOVE: Another view of No. 46202 in 1949 showing the shorter reverse turbine housing on the right-hand running plate. RAIL PHOTOPRINTS

Having gathered useful experience with the Beyer-Ljungström steam turbine locomotive (see page 27) in the mid-1920s, the LMS returned to this technology under William Stanier almost a decade later.

When his first two 'Princess Royal' 4-6-2s, Nos. 6200/01, were constructed at Crewe Works, a third set of frames was cut at the same time and used as the basis for an experimental steam turbine locomotive that became known as the 'Turbomotive'.

Taking its place in the 'Princess Royal' number series as No. 6202, the locomotive certainly looked more conventional than the Anglo-Swedish machine of the 1920s, and had a similar domeless boiler to the 1935 batch of ten additional 'Princesses' (Nos. 6204-13) but was very different below the running plate.

Using steam turbines rather than conventional cylinders, No. 6202 could be easily distinguished by the long forward turbine housing along the left-hand side of the boiler. On the right-hand side, the much smaller reverse turbine was located alongside the smokebox. Turbines were supplied by Sweden's Ljungström company, which had also been involved in the earlier Beyer, Peacock prototype (see page 24).

The forward turbine had 18 rows of blading, driven by a 250psi boiler. Maximum output was 2,400hp at

7,060rpm, or approximately 62mph. The turbine was designed to operate into a maximum back-pressure of 2psi, allowing a conventional double blastpipe and chimney to provide the boiler draught, therefore eliminating the troublesome draught fans which had added to the complexity of earlier steam turbine prototypes.

The reverse turbine had four rows of blades and could be engaged by a dog clutch, activated when the reverser was set to '0'. It was originally operated by a small steam piston and cylinder.

It entered service in June 1935 alongside its conventional sisters on the London Euston-Liverpool Lime Street route.

Unlike many other experimental steam locomotives, 'Turbomotive' was relatively successful, and saw a good deal of use on revenue-earning passenger trains between 1935 and 1949. In operation it proved to be more fuel-efficient than standard reciprocating engines and as there was no 'hammer blow' on the track from reciprocating parts it was kinder on the track and civil engineering. To overcome the disadvantages of steam turbines for railway operation, as opposed to maritime use where they generally run at constant speeds, power was controlled by a number of nozzles (from the six available) through which steam was admitted to the turbine. One disadvantage was that the smaller

reverse turbine only had sufficient power for light engine movements and No. 6202 always had to be turned to haul a train using the forward turbine. However, this was standard practice for all express locomotives, so less of a disadvantage than it would have been for a small or medium tank locomotive, for example.

Compared to its sisters, No. 6202 (No. 46202 after 1948) spent more time out of service when repairs were required as the turbine parts took longer to obtain. When a turbine failure occurred in 1949, BR's London Midland Region considered it uneconomic to repair this complex one-off machine at a time of severe post-war austerity and it was taken out of service.

However, that was not the end of No. 46202. In 1952 it was rebuilt as a conventional four-cylinder 'Pacific' using new frames and 'Princess Coronation' boiler and cylinders. This rebuild made it, for a short time, the most powerful locomotive in the country.

For the first time it also gained a name, being christened *Princess Anne* when it return to traffic that August. Sadly, just two months later it was destroyed in the Harrow & Wealdstone collision on October 8, 1952. Written off by BR as beyond economic repair, its place in the West Coast Main Line fleet was later taken by another one-off machine, BR Standard '8P' 4-6-2 No. 71000 *Duke of Gloucester*. ●

▶

ABOVE: In August 1952, during its brief period as a conventional 'Pacific', a freshly rebuilt No. 46202 *Princess Anne* passes Halton Junction with a Liverpool-Euston express. Despite receiving a 'Princess Coronation' boiler that made it Britain's most powerful locomotive, No. 46202 retained its smaller Stanier tender, restricting it to shorter duties requiring less coal and water. RAIL PHOTOPRINTS

ABOVE: An action shot of No. 46202 passing Sutton Weaver in 1949, clearly showing the main forward turbine housing along the left-hand side, the absence of external cylinders and reciprocating valve gear and the standard Stanier tender. RAIL PHOTOPRINTS

ABOVE: In its original experimental form, LNER 'W1' 4-6-4 No. 10000 leaves Grantham with the Up 'Flying Scotsman' in July 1931. T.G. HEPBURN/RAIL ARCHIVE STEPHENSON

ABOVE: An official works portrait of No. 6399 *Fury* in the 1930s, showing the massive construction of the high-pressure boiler. However, the locomotive retains much of the character of its standard 'Royal Scot' sisters. RAILWAY MAGAZINE ARCHIVE

Fury by Name…

Built to test the viability of high-pressure 'super power' steam locomotives, this experimental LMS 4-6-0 did not succeed in original form but went on to become the first of the highly capable rebuilt 'Royal Scots'.

ABOVE: Another view of No. 6399 in works photographic grey. Some doubt remains as to whether the locomotive was ever painted LMS crimson or remained in this condition until it was rebuilt. RAILWAY MAGAZINE ARCHIVE

ABOVE: Eventually patience ran out with the high-pressure boiler and William Stanier selected No. 6399 as the 'guinea pig' for rebuilding all 70 'Royal Scots' (and 20 'Patriots' and 'Jubilees') with more efficient tapered boilers. In 1935 it emerged from Crewe Works as No. 6170 *British Legion*. This view clearly shows the longer firebox fitted on this locomotive, but not on the subsequent rebuilds. RAIL PHOTOPRINTS

As we have seen over the last few pages, engineers and railway companies all over the world were constantly looking for ways to improve steam traction in the late-19th and early-20th centuries. As trains got heavier and schedules were accelerated, the demands on locomotives increased and ever more power was needed. While larger machines were part of the answer, new technologies promised to deliver greater efficiency and greater power within the existing infrastructure – this was particularly important in Britain, where the early Victorian loading gauge was much smaller than that found in mainland Europe and North America.

In 1929, the North British Locomotive Co. completed No. 6399 *Fury* for the London Midland & Scottish Railway (LMS) at its Hyde Park works in Glasgow. A joint venture between the LMS, led by Chief Mechanical Engineer Henry Fowler, NBL and The Superheater Company, *Fury* combined 'Royal Scot' running gear and frames with a complex high-pressure boiler. The name was previously carried by LMS No. 6138, which had been renamed *The London Irish Rifleman* in October 1929.

The latter company was responsible for constructing a complex, three-stage Schmidt-based boiler with many fittings imported from Germany. Specialist steelmaker John Brown & Co. of Sheffield forged a special nickel-steel alloy high pressure boiler barrel, all of which was assembled by NBL.

At the time, a number of countries around the world were investigating the potential for saving fuel and achieving greater power by using high-pressure steam, which offers greater thermodynamic efficiency than conventional low-pressure steam. Outwardly similar to a conventional Fowler 'Royal Scot', No. 6399 was a three-cylinder, semi-compound locomotive with one 11.5in high-pressure cylinder between the frames and two 18in low-pressure

outside cylinders. The Schmidt boiler was a three-stage unit with fully sealed ultra-high-pressure circuit working at 1,400 to 1,800psi. It was filled with distilled water that transferred heat from the firebox to the high-pressure drum. This raised high-pressure steam at 900psi to power the cylinders. The third steam raising unit was a relatively conventional tubed boiler operating at 250psi and heated by combustion gases from the firebox.

The first test runs were made in January 1930, followed by a longer test from Glasgow to Carstairs on February 10, 1930. However, as the train was approaching Carstairs at slow speed, one of the ultra-high-pressure tubes burst. The escaping UHP steam ejected the coal fire through the firehole door, killing the footplate representative of The Superheater Company.

The burst tube was investigated by the University of Sheffield but no definitive conclusion reached and the boiler was

eventually repaired. *Fury* moved to Derby from where running trials continued until early-1934, revealing significant shortcomings in No. 6399's performance.

France's PLM Railway also tested a locomotive with a Schmidt system HP boiler, a 4-8-2 numbered 241B1, and in 1933 it too suffered a burst ultra-high-pressure tube. It is thought that inadequate water circulation in the UHP circuit was responsible for both this and the Carstairs incident.

The locomotive was then set aside until 1935 when it was rebuilt under the supervision of Fowler's successor, William Stanier, at Crewe Works. A more conventional Type 2 tapered boiler was fitted as a prototype for the rebuilding of the entire 'Royal Scot' class, which had never lived up to LMS expectations. No. 6399 became No. 6170 *British Legion*, the first of 90 LMS 4-6-0s rebuilt and much-improved by fitting Type 2/2A boilers.

In January 1932, Stanier had replaced Fowler but showed much less interest in *Fury* than his predecessor and did not devote much time to developing the locomotive and rectifying its faults. His attention was focused elsewhere, primarily on modernising the LMS locomotive fleet with new standard designs but also on the development of his own experimental steam locomotive, the turbine-driven No. 6202 'Turbomotive'.

Despite the tragic accident at Carstairs, *Fury* was regarded as an economic rather than a technological failure. While HP boilers did indeed offer improved efficiency, they also introduced greater complexity and therefore higher maintenance costs which offset the savings made on fuel.

Fury never hauled a revenue-earning train for the LMS and is said to have travelled more miles under tow than under its own steam. However, it did provide the British locomotive builders with valuable experience of HP steam and, eventually, became the first of Stanier's very successful taper-boiler 4-6-0 rebuilds. ●

GERMANY'S HP EXPERIMENT
Deutsche Reichsbahn in Germany was also keen to investigate the potential fuel savings and increased power of high-pressure boilers and tested a remarkable 'Pacific' built by Schwartzkopff in 1929/30. Like *Fury*, No. H02 1001 did not deliver the expected increases in efficiency to justify its extra cost and complexity and it also proved to be hopelessly unreliable. ROBERT HUMM COLLECTION

Hush-Hush: Gresley's High Pressure Experiment

Nicknamed 'Hush-Hush' by works staff during its secretive development, LNER No. 10000 brought marine boiler technology to Britain's railways for the first and only time.

ABOVE: A magnificent portrait of LNER No. 10000 at Doncaster in 1930, showing the unusual shape (in railway terms) of the Yarrow marine boiler and the semi-streamlined front end.
RAIL PHOTOPRINTS

In the drive to create more efficient steam locomotives, many different ideas were tested in the first half of the 20th century. As we saw on the previous pages, a great deal of effort was directed at high-pressure boilers, which were predicted to deliver higher power and greater fuel efficiency than conventional steam traction.

At the end of 1924, the USA's American Locomotive Co. (Alco) produced the world's first main line locomotive with a marine type high-pressure water-tube boiler. This 2-8-0 goods locomotive, No. 1400

Horatio Allen, was built for the Delaware & Hudson Railroad. It used two-cylinder compound expansion and had a 350psi boiler, built by Alco with assistance from Clyde shipbuilder Yarrow & Co. Alco built three more locomotives with successive increases in boiler pressure, culminating with No. 1403 which had a boiler pressure of 500psi and is thought to have been the most thermally efficient steam locomotive ever built. However efficient they were, the locomotives were said to lack power and additional maintenance costs proved to be

higher than the savings made on fuel.

Nevertheless, the concept attracted the interest of LNER Chief Mechanical Engineer Nigel Gresley, who was keen to reduce the coal consumption of his 'Pacific' locomotives as a result of their performance in the 1923 Locomotive Interchange trials. Work started in 1924 on designs for a 'Pacific' locomotive using a marine type water tube boiler.

Between 1924 and 1927, Gresley worked with Yarrow's on a new water-tube boiler for railway locomotives. The design consisted of a long steam drum, and four water drums

ABOVE: Unlike many of the more unconventional prototypes, No. 10000 was given the opportunity to haul scheduled main line expresses. On its good days it was said to be the equal of 'a good 'A3''. On July 31, 1930 it was given the prestige duty of hauling the Down 'Flying Scotsman', captured here by a press photographer making its exit from London King's Cross.
GETTY IMAGES

connected to the steam drum via a series of tubes through which water circulated.

Gresley initially intended the boiler for a three-cylinder express passenger 'Pacific', a design for which was completed in April 1926, but this was soon modified to incorporate a fourth cylinder, repositioned furnace (firebox) and the replacement of the standard Cartazzi trailing truck with a two-axle bogie.

By 1927, the boiler pressure was also increased from 350psi to 450psi, and the requirement for the low-pressure cylinders was reduced to 200psi. In June 1927 the change of wheel arrangement to 4-6-4 was confirmed to eliminate excessive rear overhang and heavy loading on the trailing axle. As the rear bogie was partially articulated, with the first axle in an 'A1' type trailing axle and the rear axle a pony truck, the 'W1' was more correctly a 4-6-2-2, rather than a 4-6-4.

Squeezing the massive water-tube boiler into the British loading gauge proved to be a real challenge, but work

continued throughout 1928 and 1929 under top secret conditions that led to the locomotive's 'Hush-Hush' nickname.

By February 1929, the boiler had been completed and attached to the smokebox and wind tunnel experiments were undertaken to establish a suitable front end design. Boiler tests were completed by October 1929, and the partially assembled 'W1' was transferred to Darlington Works, sheeted over to hide its identity.

Completed in November 1929, the locomotive – now allocated LNER No. 10000 – made its first run on December 12 of that year, before embarking on six months of main line trials.

Out in the real world, a number of problems were identified with the 'W1' as built. Modifications were made in April 1930, including reducing the size of the superheater elements, better injectors, a reduction in the blastpipe diameter and maximum cut-off for the high-pressure valve gear was increased to 90% with a corresponding increase in the valve travel.

After further tests to prove the effectiveness of the alterations, No. 10000 entered passenger service on June 20, 1930.

By August, No. 10000 was back at Darlington Works for repairs to a leaking regulator valve, caused by bent operating levers. The opportunity was taken to make further modifications, including another replacement superheater, keeping it out of traffic until January 1931. Over the next two years the locomotive made regular works visits for unscheduled repairs and tests, including measuring pressure, temperature, and carbon dioxide emissions.

In May 1933, No. 10000 reached the 70,000 mile mark and returned to Darlington Works for its first general repair and more modifications.

The blastpipe diameter was reduced, again, from 4.75in to 4.25in, and its height lowered by 2.5in. Condensation in the low-pressure cylinders proved to be a problem when the engine was stationary. Legendary French steam locomotive engineer, and Gresley's friend, Andre Chapelon ▶

ABOVE: After No. 10000 was rebuilt as a streamlined 4-6-2-2 with a stretched 'A1' boiler in 1937, its marine boiler was put to good use at Stooperdale Works in Darlington. It was finally scrapped in 1965, outliving No. 10000 by six years. RAILWAY MAGAZINE ARCHIVE

ABOVE: The rebuilt No. 10000 at King's Cross Top Shed in 1938. Only the extended cab and extra trailing axle beneath distinguish it from a garter blue 'A4'. RAIL PHOTOPRINTS

Darlington Works for general repairs and further modifications. However, Gresley put a stop to the experiment at this point and in 1936/37 No. 10000 was rebuilt with a conventional fire-tube boiler and 'A4' style streamlined casing at Doncaster Works, re-emerging in November 1937.

In rebuilt form, the locomotive retained its 4-6-2-2 wheel arrangement but was converted to three-cylinder form with a stretched 250psi 'A1' boiler similar to that fitted to 'P2/2' No. 2006 *Wolf of Badenoch*. As much as possible of the original locomotive was kept, including the frames which had to be shortened by 18in.

No. 10000 retained its number under Thompson's 1943 renumbering scheme, but was renumbered as No. 60700 by British Railways in 1948. As a singleton with a unique boiler, the 'W1' tended to spend longer in works than standard LNER 'Pacifics', alongside which it ran until withdrawal on June 1, 1959.

In a commendable piece of recycling, the water-tube boiler was sent back to Darlington and used for pressure testing and space heating at Stooperdale boiler works until 1965, outliving the rebuilt 'W1' by almost six years.

The complexities of the unique boiler, more suited to the constant power demands of marine operation, meant that the locomotive was considerably more expensive to build and more expensive to maintain than conventional steam locomotives. Of the 1,888 days since it was completed in 1929, the locomotive is said to have spent no fewer than 1,105 days at Darlington Works undergoing tests, repair or modification. However, although Gresley's revolutionary design is generally regarded as a failure, No. 10000 did successfully run in revenue-earning service with the LNER, and by the time development work stopped was regarded as the equal of a good 'A3'.

For more information on LNER No. 10000, see *Hush-Hush: The Story of LNER 10000* by William Brown (Kestrel Books, 2010) ●

recommended that exhaust from the high-pressure cylinders should be re-superheated before being re-used in the low-pressure cylinders. As a result, Gresley ordered the installation of an intermediate superheater.

Other modifications included the addition of aluminium foil insulation between the boiler and the casing and the addition of tubes connecting the front and rear water drums. No. 10000 returned to service in June 1934.

Chapelon also recommended changing the exhaust arrangement to the Kylchap design first applied to LNER 'P2' 2-8-2 No. 2001 *Cock O'The North* in 1934. No. 10000 followed suit in 1935, although its very different design required a number of adjustments in May/June 1935 before a satisfactory arrangement was found.

By August 1935, the 'W1' had completed around 90,000 miles and was back at

Soviet High Pressure 0-4-4T

Another unusual prototype from the Soviet Union was B5-01, built by Kolomna in 1937. Fitted with a very high-pressure boiler, it is thought to have been the last 0-4-4T locomotive built anywhere in the world. ROBERT HUMM COLLECTION

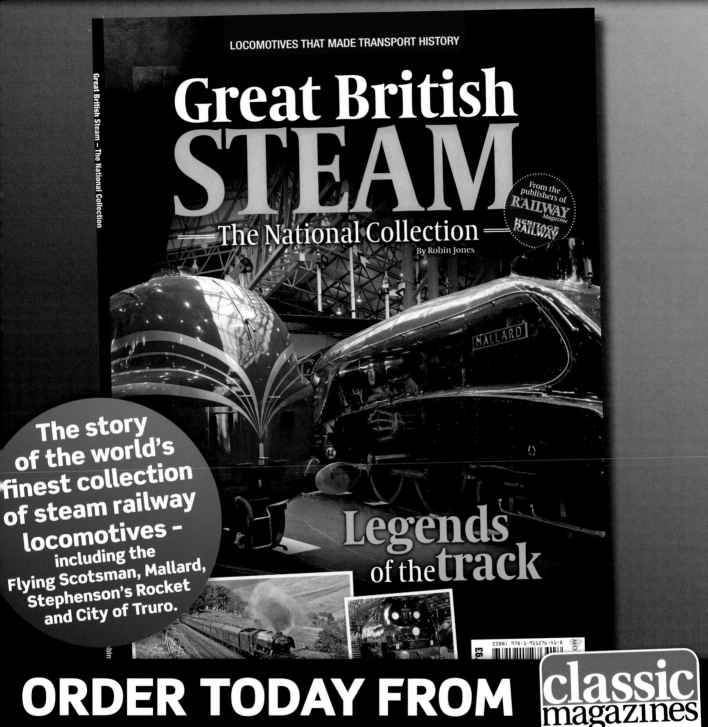 

Getting a Boost

In the 1920s and 1930s, the LNER experimented with boosters to increase the starting power of passenger and heavy goods locomotives. The 'booster' was a secondary steam engine attached to trailing or tender axles for use at low speeds.

ABOVE: Even before the Grouping of 1923, Nigel Gresley was investigating the possibilities offered by booster engines. Ex-GNER Ivatt 'Atlantic' No. 4419 was the first locomotive to be rebuilt, in 1923, gaining a small two-cylinder engine attached to the rear trailing axle. Despite extensive trials and refinements, it suffered from mechanical failures and poor riding and was removed in 1935. RAIL PHOTOPRINTS

ABOVE: Despite the problems with No. 4419, the results of the trial were encouraging enough to persuade Gresley to fit his two new 'P1' heavy mineral 2-8-2s with booster equipment in 1925. Testing showed that the booster was only effective with loads of 1,600t or greater – much more than was typical at the time. Other problems included leaking steam pipes so the boosters were removed in 1937/38. RAIL PHOTOPRINTS

ABOVE: Booster-fitted locomotives were also tested at the busy hump marshalling yard at Wath in South Yorkshire, where standard locomotives struggled to maintain adhesion in wet weather. One of the four former Great Central Railway Robinson 'S1/2' 0-8-4Ts (No. 6171) was rebuilt in 1931/32 and two further 'S1/3s' were built to the same design in 1932, working at Wath, and later at Whitemoor in Cambridgeshire. The boosters were removed in 1943 to simplify maintenance. LNER-built 'S1/3' No. 2799 sits at Mexborough, its home shed, in 1930. RAIL PHOTOPRINTS

ABOVE: An official works view of one of the two former North Eastern Railway 'C7' 4-4-2s, No. 727, which was rebuilt as a booster-fitted 4-4-4-4 along with No. 2171 in 1932. Unlike the other LNER conversions, the 'C9s' were designed to provide extra power up to 30mph and reduce the need for double-heading of trains between Newcastle and Edinburgh. RAILWAY MAGAZINE ARCHIVE

ABOVE: LNER 'C9' No. 727 at York in 1937. With regular crews the booster equipment is reported to have worked well but fell into disuse when the 'C9s' became common-user machines and was removed in late-1936/early-1937. The two non-standard locomotives were withdrawn in 1942/43. RAIL PHOTOPRINTS ●

Improving the Breed

For more than 150 years, engineers across the world tried to find ways to improve on Stephenson's model, trying to increase the efficiency, power and speed of steam traction. Some were successful, others less so, and the ideas ranged from simple and effective to downright bizarre!

ABOVE: In September 1903, Great Northern Railway Locomotive Superintendent H.A. Ivatt fitted this extraordinary appendage to Stirling 2-4-0 No. 708. Recorded as Druitt-Halpin thermal storage apparatus, it was carried by the Kitson-built locomotive until September 1908. H.L. HOPWOOD/RAILWAY MAGAZINE ARCHIVE

LEFT: Very few British railway companies bought steam locomotives from foreign suppliers, but in 1903/05, the GWR took delivery of three de Glehn/du Bosquet four-cylinder compound 4-4-2s from SACM in France. They were similar to the Paris-Orleans Railway's '3001' class and bought to evaluate the benefits of compounding. By 1922, No. 104 *Alliance* had been 'Swindonised' with a GWR No. 1 boiler. RAIL PHOTOPRINTS

ABOVE: Steam railmotors were introduced by numerous British railways in the late-19th and early 20th century to reduce operating costs on lightly used lines and short-distance shuttles. Great Northern Railway No. 6 combines a very small 0-4-0T steam locomotive with a teak-bodied saloon. Other railways used vertical-boiler locomotives, including the GWR which had a large fleet of railmotors in the 1900s. RAIL PHOTOPRINTS

ABOVE: Best-known for its steam lorries, the Sentinel Waggon Works of Shrewsbury also built various steam rail vehicles with vertical boilers and chain/gear driven power bogies. LMS Sentinel-Cammell steam railcar No. 29910 was one of several prototypes built and tested by different companies. Similar cars were built for use in Jersey and further afield, while the LNER had a large fleet of Sentinel and Clayton steam railcars. COLOUR-RAIL

ABOVE: The earliest known image of a steam railcar is this view of 1849-built inspection car *Eagle* at Stratford Works in east London in the 1860s. RAILWAY MAGAZINE ARCHIVE

ABOVE: LMS No. 7192 was an experimental geared steam locomotive fitted with an Abner-Doble vertical boiler and four-cylinder compound arrangement. It was built in 1934 for comparative tests against the various types of new diesel shunter then being introduced. However, it was not a success and orders for another machine and three railcars with similar technology were cancelled. No. 7192 was scrapped in 1943. COLOUR-RAIL

ABOVE: Under Nigel Gresley's direction, the LNER tested various types of equipment designed to increase the efficiency of steam locomotives. Several older classes acted as testbeds for equipment such as the ACFI feed water heating apparatus fitted to 'B12' 4-6-0 No. 8507 and seen at Stratford MPD in 1936. RAIL PHOTOPRINTS

▶

ABOVE & BELOW: After the LNER and LMS scored major publicity successes with their streamlined trains of the late-1930s, GWR Chief Mechanical Engineer Charles Collett came under pressure to produce his own streamlined machines. The less-than-convincing results were 'Castle' No. 5005 *Manorbier Castle* and 'King' No. 6014 *King Henry VII*, both captured at Old Oak Common on September 28, 1935. RAIL PHOTOPRINTS (2)

ABOVE: In response to faster electric services being planned in competition with its own trains from Liverpool Street, the Great Eastern Railway built a one-off 0-10-0T prototype in 1902. It was designed to prove that steam traction could accelerate away from frequent station stops as quickly as electric trains and was the first British ten-coupled locomotive. However, it was not a success and was rebuilt as an 0-8-0 goods locomotive in 1906 and scrapped in 1913. RAILWAY MAGAZINE ARCHIVE

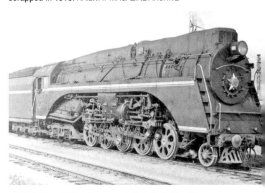

ABOVE: In 1948, British Railways built 20 modified Stanier 'Black Fives' (Nos. 44738-57) with Caprotti valvegear, rather than the standard Walschaerts arrangement as part of an experimental programme by H.G. Ivatt to improve an already proven design. No. 44739 passes Helsby with a lightweight express in 1949, representing the original Caprotti '5MT' look, while No. 44687 at Patricroft in September 1960 illustrates the quite different appearance of the final two of 842 'Black Fives' built, in 1951, with externally-mounted rotary British Caprotti valve gear and SKF roller bearings throughout. RAIL PHOTOPRINTS (2)

ABOVE: Many different proposals for eliminating the destructive 'hammer blow' forces of reciprocating steam locomotives, including steam turbines and balanced opposing pistons, however most were too complex for everyday service. Soviet Railways OR23-01 was an opposed piston 2-10-4 built in 1949 by Voroshilovgrad, but it too was a failure and never worked in revenue earning service. ROBERT HUMM COLLECTION

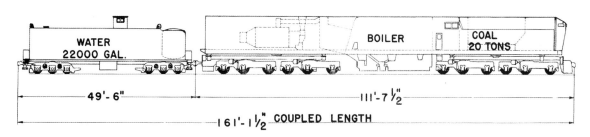

WATER
22000 GAL.

BOILER

COAL
20 TONS

49'-6"

111'-7½"

161'-1½" COUPLED LENGTH

July 1954 THE LOCOMOTIVE

NORFOLK & WESTERN RAILWAY
COAL-FIRED STEAM TURBINE, ELECTRIC DRIVE 6-6-6-6 LOCOMOTIVE NO. 2300

Starting tractive effort 175,000 lb.; Rated continuous tractive effort (9 m.p.h.) 144,000 lb.; Rated maximum speed 60 m.p.h.; Weight in working order, locomotive 807,000 lb. (all adhesive); Tender 365,000 lb. Wheelbase, rigid 13ft.; total engine 96ft. 5½in., engine and tender 147ft 3½in.; Driving wheel diameter 3ft. 6in.

ABOVE: Sitting on almost inexhaustible supplies of coal, the Norfolk & Western Railway persisted with steam traction far longer than many other US railroads. In 1954 Baldwin built this extraordinary 6-6-6-6 steam turbine-electric prototype rated at 4,500hp. At 161ft long it is thought to have been the longest steam locomotive ever built, but it ran for less than four years before being retired. ROBERT HUMM COLLECTION ●

Kitson-Still Steam-Diesel Hybrid

ABOVE: The unique Kitson-Still steam-diesel hybrid in the roundhouse at York shed in 1933. ROBERT HUMM COLLECTION

While diesel locomotives with electric transmission have been commonplace since the 1940s, the technology was still unproven in the 1920s, and various other new forms of traction were being devised in parallel to challenge it.

One of the most unusual to modern eyes was the Kitson-Still steam-diesel hybrid locomotive, which was tested on the LNER in 1933-34.

Proven in marine and stationary use, the Still engine featured double-acting pistons with one side operated by diesel fuel and the other by steam. The engine was started by steam, and diesel fuel was injected into the diesel side of the cylinders once the engine was running at sufficient speed – starting at around 5mph. The steam starting principle allowed direct propulsion without any form of transmission. The design also allowed steam to be used as a 'booster' when extra power was required.

Steam was then shut off until needed for the next start, or for greater power output. Maximum design speed was 43mph, later increased to 55mph as experience was gained with the locomotive on the main line.

An oil burner was used to fire up the steam boiler, and exhaust heat from the diesel engine was directed through tubes in the boiler to partially heat the steam. This recycled heat improved the thermal efficiency to about 40% - far in excess of all other locomotives of the time, especially conventional steam types which could only manage around 7%.

Leeds locomotive builder Kitson & Co. saw the potential of the Still concept for railway use and construction of an experimental 1-C-1 prototype started in 1924.

Eight cylinders were arranged in two horizontal banks, parallel with the drive axles and driving a central crankshaft.

Gears, a layshaft and coupling rods transferred power from the crankshaft to the three driven axles. A small diameter boiler with an oil-burning firebox was positioned above the engine.

After completion, tests were performed on LNER lines around Leeds and York for a number of years. The LNER showed some interest in the machine and even displayed it at an exhibition at Leeds in April 1928. Later that year, it successfully hauled a 400 ton goods train from Darlington to Starbeck (near Harrogate) and back. Impressively, it restarted its train on a 1-in-33 gradient during the test run.

By 1933, the Kitson-Still locomotive had become reliable enough to work a regular daily goods diagram from York to Hull Dairycoates and back. During this period it was based at York North shed (now the National Railway Museum).

Significantly, the locomotive consumed about one-fifth of the fuel used by a conventional steam locomotive, by weight. Kitson aimed to market the locomotive to countries with good oil supplies but no coal.

However, for an 88 ton machine with a 20t axle loading, the available power was relatively low and at the time Kitson was not in a position to invest heavily in developing the concept to improve its power-to-weight ratio. The company had already spent almost a decade and considerable sums of money developing and testing the prototype and the experimental machine is said to have been a major contributing factor to Kitson's decision to call in the receivers in 1934. As a result, the prototype was stored at York North until at least July 1935 before returning to its Leeds birthplace for disposal. By this time, diesel technology was maturing and earlier reliability problems with electric and hydraulic transmissions were being resolved, rendering this interesting experiment obsolete. ●

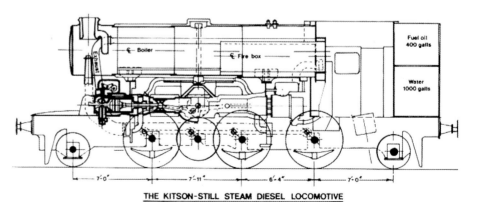

THE KITSON-STILL STEAM DIESEL LOCOMOTIVE

ABOVE: General arrangement drawing of the Kitson-Still locomotive. RAILWAY MAGAZINE ARCHIVE

Leader: Steam's Last Gasp?

Few experimental locomotives have ever proved as controversial as Oliver Bulleid's doomed attempt to overcome the operational disadvantages of steam against its diesel and electric counterparts.

ABOVE: No. 36001 at Brighton shed in 1950. In March 1951, BR quietly cancelled the project, putting an end to Bulleid's brave attempt to make steam traction relevant for the post-war era. COLOUR-RAIL

B y the 1940s, it was becoming increasingly obvious that the steam locomotive's days as the primary form of railway traction were coming to an end. Diesel and electric traction had proved their worth after several decades of gradual development and were seen as clean, efficient and less labour intensive than dirty, polluting steam locomotives.

However, not everyone agreed that steam was doomed, and work continued to make steam locomotives more efficient, more powerful and easier to operate, especially in countries with large reserves of good quality coal. In Britain, Southern Railway Chief Mechanical Engineer O.V.S. Bulleid was already well-known for his innovative approach to locomotive and rolling stock design, which had produced a series of 'Pacific' locomotives with highly efficient boilers, improvements to existing SR steam types, the unusual 'Q1' goods 0-6-0 and a range of modern suburban electric trains.

In 1946, design work began on his next new locomotive, intended to replace vintage Drummond 'M7' 0-4-4Ts on branch line and secondary work away from the electrified network. Rather than producing a modern passenger tank, as other railways had done, Bulleid set out to extend the life of steam traction by eliminating many of the operational drawbacks associated with conventional locomotives. Development continued after Nationalisation in 1948 and the first locomotive was completed at Brighton Works in June 1949. Although ▶

ABOVE: No. 36001 was the only 'Leader' to be completed and run under its own power. Brighton Works staff put the final touches to the locomotive in 1949. COLOUR-RAIL

ABOVE: A much more work-stained No. 36001 dumped outside Eastleigh Works in October 1950. This angle highlights the massive construction of the bogies and the position of the cramped fireman's compartment towards the far end of the locomotive. RAIL PHOTOPRINTS

five locomotives were started, only No. 36001 was completed and ever ran under its own power. A 1947 SR order for 31 more 'Leaders' was cancelled immediately after Nationalisation.

Originally proposed as a development of the 'Q1' in 1944, the design progressed to become an 0-4-0+0-4-0T and then an 0-6-0+0-6-0T to reduce its axleload and increase its route availability. The design incorporated many novel features, such as the use of lighter Bulleid-Firth-Brown 'Boxpok' wheels, thermic siphons and chain drives running in oil baths (as used on Bulleid's 'Pacifics'), bogies and driving cabs at each end, producing something more akin to a diesel locomotive, externally at least.

The cabs allowed drivers a much better view of the road ahead and eliminated the need for turntables at each end of routes.

The boiler was offset to provide space for a corridor, allowing the driver to access both cabs without leaving the locomotive. However, the fireman was condemned to work in a sweltering, claustrophobic and often dangerous enclosed third cab by the firebox in the middle of the locomotive.

Each bogie had three cylinders using sleeve valves first seen on the Paget locomotive in 1908 (see page 22) and fitted by Bulleid as a trial on ex-LBSCR 'H1' 4-4-2 No. 2039 *Hartland Point.*

One innovative feature of the steam bogie assembly was the ability to swap them when faults occurred, an easy operation for maintenance staff compared to the complexities of maintaining and repairing conventional steam locomotive motion.

While components such as the oil baths, sleeve valves and smokebox were problematic, leading many modifications during the test programme, once again Bulleid's boiler design proved to be the strongest aspect of the concept.

No. 36001 operated a number of trial runs with empty coaching stock in the south-east of England. Official Brighton Works documents report varying degrees of success and failure but the results of the trials as reported to BR headquarters were unfavourable, highlighting problems with the boiler, braking system and adhesion provided by the two bogies. It has been suggested that the more conservative forces at Brighton Works and within the Railway Executive felt that the 'Leader' was too revolutionary and were keen to develop more conventional machines.

However, out on the road, No. 36001 displayed numerous flaws, including heavy coal and water consumption, mechanical unreliability, impossible working conditions for crews, loss of steam through the cylinder rings and uneven weight distribution on the bogies. The firebrick lining of the firebox was also a constant problem, continually collapsing into the fire. Cast-iron replacements melted in the heat.

The offset boiler and coal bunker shifted the locomotive's centre of gravity to one side and large quantities of scrap metal were dropped in in an effort to correct it. The ballast weight was later covered by a steel plate in a redesign of the interior, but this boosted the overall weight to a whopping 150 tons, severely limiting the 'Leader's' route availability.

Despite its problems, the locomotive displayed outstanding steaming characteristics and total traction from the bogies during trial runs. In the right hands, the 'Leader' was capable of maintaining schedules, even beating them on occasions but difficulties in replenishing the water tanks tended to dissipate any advantages gained.

No. 36001 never hauled a revenue-earning train because of the risk of failure of the valve gear and the adverse publicity it would generate for BR. In March 1951, BR quietly cancelled the project, putting an end to Bulleid's brave attempt to make steam traction relevant for the post-war era.

Nos. 36002–005 were at varying stages of construction by the end of the development period. No. 36002 was almost complete, No. 36003 was without its outer casing, and Nos. 36004–005 were little more than sets of frames, although most of their major components had been constructed at Eastleigh and Brighton and were stored ready for assembly. With no prospect of further money being allocated by the Railway Executive for their completion, the unfinished locomotives were put into store around the former SR network and eventually scrapped.

Despite his high expectations, the 'Leader' was not the motive power revolution that Bulleid intended. By this time, he had left BR to become Chief Mechanical Engineer of Córas Iompair Éireann in Ireland, where he produced CIÉ No. CC1, a peat-burning locomotive similar in concept to the 'Leader' (see panel).

Officially, the failed project had cost almost £179,000 (more than £5.5m at current prices) although in 1953 a figure more than three times that was reported as being wasted on the project. ●

ROBERT HUMM COLLECTION

BULLEID'S TURF BURNER

Having resigned from the Southern Region in 1949, O.V.S. Bulleid moved to Córas Iompair Éireann (CIÉ) in Ireland, taking up the post of Consulting Engineer, later CME, at Inchicore Works in Dublin.

Irish railways had experimented with turf (peat) as a source of fuel since the mid-19th century as, unlike steam coal, it was plentiful in the country and much cheaper than imported fuel.

The Second World War, known as 'the Emergency' in Ireland and the harsh winter of 1946/47 exposed Ireland's over-dependence on imported Welsh coal and CIÉ committed to dieselisation to overcome this. However, Bulleid was concerned about Ireland's ability to afford an entire fleet of new diesels and gained permission to design a new steam locomotive able to run exclusively on Irish turf.

Various experiments were undertaken using a former Great Southern Railway 'Woolwich' 2-6-0 (a broad gauge version of Maunsell's 'N' Class), and lessons drawn from the 'Leader' project leading to the construction of CC1, a 68ft long 0-6-6-0 with strong external similarities to the 'Leader'.

The rather unattractive external casing hid a complex arrangement of hoppers, blowers and pre-heating piping required to extract the maximum energy from the turf. The central boiler was flanked by a water tank at one end and the turf hopper at the other, holding around eight tons of fuel.

The bogies were of lighter construction than massive 'Leader' units, with chain drive but only two cylinders per bogie and Walschaerts valve gear rather than the problematic sleeve valves. Reports from the time suggested CC1 had more success than the 'Leader', although further development was required to make it suitable for revenue service. It was first steamed in 1957 and ran main line trials that summer on the Dublin-Cork main line, making it as far as Cork on two occasions. Speeds of up to 70mph were attained, and the ride qualities, fuel consumption and noise levels were also reported to be favourable. However, there were various problems, including high water consumption, lineside fires caused by still-burning turf being ejected from the exhaust (cured by the fitting of spark arrestors), boiler problems, visibility issues caused by drifting smoke and leaking oil baths, a problem common to all Bulleid steam locomotives.

Although CC1 was intended to be the basis of a class of 50 production turf burners, by the time Bulleid retired in 1958, CIÉ had more than 100 imported diesel locomotives in service and development work on CC1 ceased. It was officially withdrawn in 1963 but parts of the locomotive survived until at least the mid-1970s. ●

ABOVE: An almost new No. 92026 shows off its unconventional configuration in the mid-1950s. Below the smokebox, the extra door for the pre-heater drum is visible. The side-mounted chimney is also prominent – a smoke deflector was fitted later to reduce the amount of smoke drifting into the cab. RAILWAY MAGAZINE ARCHIVE

BR '9F' Experiments

Although they proved to be among the best of the BR Standard steam types, the '9F' 2-10-0s were subject to several experiments in the 1950s as BR attempted to make its fleet more efficient.

LEFT: Ten '9Fs', Nos. 92020-029, were built with Franco-Crosti boilers which promised more efficient operation and fuel savings. Unfortunately the locomotives proved to be dirty and unreliable and were eventually rebuilt with standard boilers. Visitors to Crewe Works inspect the new No. 92022 in March 1955. RAIL PHOTOPRINTS

ABOVE: Just seven years after the photograph above, a filthy No. 92022 is dumped in the shed yard at Wellingborough on February 18, 1962. It is stored awaiting the call to works for rebuilding. RAIL PHOTOPRINTS

ABOVE: Rebuilt 'Crosti' No. 92028 gets under way from Gloucester with a train of unfitted 16t mineral wagons on June 29, 1965. As well as removing the pre-heater drum, the modifications included moving the blastpipe and chimney to a more familiar location. RAIL PHOTOPRINTS

LEFT: Another non-standard '9F' was the Western Region's No. 92250, which was fitted with a Giesl ejector – a suction draught system invented in 1951 by Austrian engineer Dr Adolph Giesl-Gieslingen. Giesl's system replaced the standard blastpipe with several fan-shaped diverging blastpipes topped by a narrow diffuser. It promised fuel savings of 6-12% and up to 20% more power but the results with No. 92250 were reported as 'indifferent'. However, Bulleid 'Light Pacific' No. 34064 *Fighter Command* saw better results when it gained a Giesl ejector in 1962 and the system was widely used in Germany, Austria, Czechoslovakia and further afield in the 1960s and 1970s, with East Germany alone converting more than 500 locomotives. RAIL PHOTOPRINTS ●

The Quest for Economy

As their dominance was eroded by road transport in the 1920s and 1930s, railway companies looked for ways to save costs on loss-making lines and make labour intensive operations more efficient. The emerging force of the internal combustion engine offered lots of potential, but it took more than three decades to develop locomotives and railcars that could end the dominance of British steam.

Even while the railways were enjoying their heyday in the late-19th and early 20th centuries, there were clouds on the horizon. Many lines had been promoted and developed in the frenzied time of the 'railway mania' when every settlement of any size demanded a link to the network. Add to this the competition between companies for traffic in the major towns and cities and, after the First World War, the introduction of cheap, army surplus road lorries competing with the railways for goods traffic and it was inevitable that some lines would struggle to cover their costs.

While railway companies had (almost) always sought to work economically and efficiently, many of the less prosperous operators identified the need to cut costs by the early 20th century. The earliest steam railcars were built as far back as 1847 by W. Bridges Adams in Bow, East London and tested on the Eastern Counties Railway, but it was not until the brief fashion in the late-19th and early 20th century for steam railmotors – carriages with small, built-in steam locomotives or vertical boilers mounted on power bogies – that the concept became more widely known. However, these had their limitations and many of the railmotors lasted only a few years before being replaced by conventional trains or push-pull 'auto-trains' powered by standard locomotives.

However, even before the 1914-18 war, experiments were taking place that would eventually lead to a revolution in passenger trains, and much more efficient operations for secondary and branch line railways.

Experiments with petrol-electric traction in Hungary and elsewhere had attracted the attention of British engineers, but until the late-1920s development was somewhat slower in the UK than it was in continental Europe.

The North Eastern Railway (NER) was a pioneer in applying internal combustion engine technology to railway vehicles. As early as May 1903 it built two petrol-electric 'autocars', similar to the Tyneside electric stock being built at the time. Both had matchboard sides, large windows and a clerestory roof, but the autocars had an 85hp Napier engine driving a dynamo that delivered 550 Volts to two 55hp electric motors on one bogie. The power bogie, petrol engine and generator were all located at one end along with main driving controls. A smaller driving compartment was located at the opposite end of the vehicle.

Nos. 3170 and 3171 entered service in August 1904 but were not a great success, proving too heavy for the power available. They were intended to operate between Hartlepool and West Hartlepool, in competition with a local tram service. It is thought that only one car worked this ▶

ABOVE: Early internal combustion-engined railcars took many different forms as railways sought cheap vehicles to reduce costs on lightly-used lines. This replica Ford Model 'T' railbus at the Derwent Valley Light Railway's centenary celebrations in July 2013 is based on a vehicle built for use on the famous Col. Stephens light railways, including the Kent & East Sussex Railway, Selsey Tramway and the Shropshire & Montgomeryshire, but similar 'homemade' conversions were used in many countries, including the USA, Australia and New Zealand. PAUL BICKERDYKE

ABOVE: The North Eastern Railway pioneered the use of petrol-powered railcars in the 1900s, including a pair of petrol-electric vehicles based on Tyneside EMU stock. One of these vehicles survives and is being restored to working order in North Yorkshire after many years as a summer house! RAILWAY MAGAZINE ARCHIVE

route, with the other employed between Scarborough and Filey. They were tried on other routes including between Billingham and Port Clarence, near Middlesbrough and the Selby-Cawood branch.

In 1923, No. 3170 received a war surplus six-cylinder 225hp engine and a larger dynamo and received the new number 3170Y. It was then transferred to Starbeck to operate to Ripon, Wetherby, Pannal, Pateley Bridge, and Knaresborough.

During the 1920s, the two autocars appear to have been little used and No. 3171 was withdrawn in May 1930 with No. 3170Y following in April 1931.

The body of No. 3170 was sold to a North Yorkshire landowner and used as a holiday home. After many years of neglect, it was sold for preservation and is being restored to running condition at the Embsay & Bolton Abbey Railway, along with a matching NER auto-trailer.

In March 1908, the NER also built a 40hp petrol-powered inspection car at York Works. It was intended for use by NER management on inspection journeys, and had a central map table with six seats.

In 1911, NER chief mechanical engineer Vincent Raven suggested that two larger, 12-seat cars should be ordered and they were built by the NER using White & Poppe six-cylinder engines rated at 75hp. By 1929, the two oldest inspection cars were showing their age and both had new 80hp Leyland engines fitted. Although they were cheaper to run than a steam locomotive and saloon, the latter could also be used for other duties. All three railcars were withdrawn in February 1939.

Other experiments undertaken by the NER included Petrol Rail Motor Bus No. 130Y of 1922, which saw a Leyland road bus converted to run on rails. With a long bonnet and a overhanging roof at the front, it was a typical bus design of

the time. The conversion was completed at York Carriage Works and involved the addition of an extra radiator and a second driving position at the rear of the vehicle. Total seating capacity was 26 passengers.

It initially worked from York to Haxby, Strensall, Earswick, and Copmanthorpe. In July 1923 it was transferred to Selby and worked to Straddlethorpe, York, Goole, Castleford, Market Weighton, Cawood, and Hemingborough. No. 130 took part in the Stockton & Darlington Centenary celebrations in 1925, but was destroyed by fire while being fuelled at Selby shed on November 11, 1926.

Another petrol autocar, No. 2105Y, was completed at York Works in July 1923. It was powered by a six-cylinder 105hp Daimler engine and could seat 40 passengers. Unusually, it had a two axle bogie at the engine end, and a single fixed, powered axle at the other end. It was also based at York and took over from 130Y on local duties until 1930 when stations at Haxby, Strensall and Flaxton closed. It found work around Hull in 1932 but was then out of use until withdrawal in May 1934.

Between 1925 and 1932, the LNER purchased 80 Sentinel steam railcars to work rural routes across its system, a move which put an end to the NER's development of petrol/diesel railcars.

Great Central railcar

Impressed by developments elsewhere in Europe, the Great Central Railway (GCR) purchased a petrol-electric bogie railcar from Westinghouse Electric & Manufacturing Co. in Manchester in 1912. The carbody was constructed by United Electric Car Co. of Preston. The vehicle could seat 50 people but was lighter and more powerful than the NER autocars.

A 90hp six-cylinder petrol engine was located at the front but the silencer and radiator were located on the roof.

Initial trials were undertaken around Manchester, but press trips operated between Marylebone and South Harrow on March 28, 1912. It is thought to have been tested on rush-hour commuter services out of Marylebone initially, but by 1914, the railcar was based at Dinting to work the Glossop branch. From August 1921 it worked between Macclesfield Central and Bollington and was nicknamed the 'Bollington Bug'. It was withdrawn in July 1935 and replaced by a Sentinel steam railcar.

Armstrong-Whitworth Prototypes

As we will come to see over the next few pages, Newcastle engineering giant Armstrong-Whitworth was heavily involved in the early development of diesel traction for railways. In 1931, A-W designed and built a diesel-electric railcar at its own expense to demonstrate the possibilities of this technology. It was designed to demonstrate multiple-unit operation as well as railcar-trailer operations.

A 250hp Sulzer six-cylinder, four-stroke diesel engine, built under licence, was installed in the underframe at one end of the vehicle.

Two General Electric traction motors powered one bogie, giving a maximum design speed of 65mph. The carbody was built by Cravens of Sheffield. Two saloons could seat 25 passengers each with seats in a 3+2 arrangement.

This first railcar was named *Tyneside Venturer* and started a 36 week trial with the LNER on April 11, 1932. This included regular passenger workings around Newcastle and Middlesbrough.

It was purchased by the LNER on November 24 that year and officially handed over on December 12, 1932.

A second railcar, *Lady Hamilton*, ran tests on the LNER in 1932 and was purchased in 1934 along with *Northumbrian*, a third railcar which had previously been on trial with the LMS.

A fourth A-W diesel-electric vehicle entered service with the LNER in 1933. No. 294 was a lightweight railbus completed in May 1933. It underwent six months of trials before entering regular service around Newcastle in September 1933. It was taken into official LNER stock in August 1934.

No. 294 had an underfloor engine, a Saurer 95bhp diesel unit, with one traction motor mounted on the underframe to drive the leading axle of the front bogie. A streamlined body was constructed by Park Royal.

Tyneside Venturer ran 34,146 miles and used 7,087gal of fuel during its 36-week trial, recording a fuel economy of 4.82 miles per gallon. On a demonstration run from King's Cross to Newcastle in July 1932, *Lady Hamilton* recorded an average speed of 47.6mph and 6.27mpg fuel consumption. However, as the vehicles aged their performance deteriorated, possibly due to poor maintenance and a lack of experience with diesel traction.

The railcars were largely used on former NER routes, but *Tyneside Venturer* was also trialled on ex-GNR lines in West Yorkshire in 1935.

All three railcars were stored at Darlington in 1939 pending a decision on their future. They are thought to have been scrapped during 1944, but provided a great deal of information and experience on the construction and operation of diesel railcars that influenced the later development of such vehicles.

LMS Experiments

Europe's first diesel-electric passenger train was a four-car LMS set converted in 1928 from one of the former Lancashire & Yorkshire Railway (LYR) 3.5kV DC third-rail experimental EMUs used on the Bury-Holcombe Brook line. Fitted with a 500hp Beardmore engine and Dick, Kerr electrical components it was not a success but it did encourage Dick, Kerr's parent company, English Electric, to start developing its own diesel engines for rail traction.

The LMS also tested an unusual ten-wheeled, rubber-tyred railcar built by the Michelin Tyre Co. in France in 1932. During tests on the Bedford-Bicester line it covered the run in 30 minutes at an average speed of 38.5mph, compared to the 42 minutes of a normal steam-hauled train and returned from Oxford to Bletchley in 41min at an average speed of 45.5mph. Fuel economy of 12mpg was also claimed. Michelin was also tested on the Southern Railway and a second, more advanced vehicle ran on the LNER but no orders were placed on this side of the Channel. However, various experimental 'Micheline'

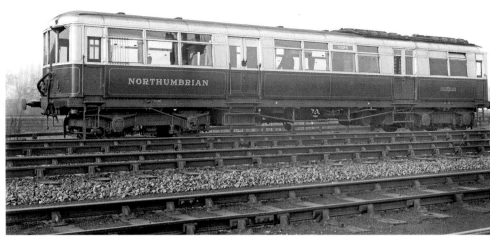

ABOVE: *Northumbrian* was one of four diesel-electric railcars built by Armstrong-Whitworth in 1931-33 and tested extensively by the LNER and LMS. RAILWAY MAGAZINE ARCHIVE

ABOVE: In 1939 the LMS produced a very fine streamlined articulated three-piece diesel railcar. It was heavily influenced by the LMS (NCC) railcars in Northern Ireland, using identical engines and transmission as NCC Nos. 2–4. It had six engines producing a total of 750hp and could run at up to 75mph. COLOUR-RAIL

vehicles did run in France and several lines of the Paris Metro employ rubber-tyred trains using similar technology.

Separately, the LMS bought three four-wheel diesel railcars from Leyland in 1933. Nos. 29950–952 each had a 95hp diesel engine. After trials between Preston and Carlisle they worked around Blackburn and Hamilton in Scotland. Although they passed to BR in 1948 they had been withdrawn by 1951, but the 4w railcar concept would make several comebacks over the next four decades.

Another unusual LMS diesel vehicle was the Karrier Road-Railer tested in 1932 on the rural Stratford-upon-Avon and Midland Junction Railway (SMJR). Combining a standard road bus body with pneumatic rubber tyres and flanged rail wheels, it could be used both on

rails and on the road. However, the tests were not a success and the bus ran for just a few weeks before a major failure caused it to be returned to Wolverton Works and never used in service again.

Altogether more sophisticated was a three-car articulated railcar outshopped from Derby Works in 1939. Nos. 80000/001/002 formed a streamlined three-car unit with two 64ft long driving cars and 52ft centre vehicle. Articulation had previously been employed on locomotive-hauled stock by LMS Chief Mechanical Engineer Sir William Stanier on front-line express passenger coaches. Mechanically the train was heavily influenced by the LMS (NCC) railcars in Northern Ireland (see above), using identical engines and transmission as NCC Nos. 2–4. Two vertically mounted ▶

ABOVE: Another unusual lightweight railcar tested by the LMS was the Michelin Tyre Co.'s rubber-tyred Micheline. Similar vehicles were tried in France, including high-speed railcars and express carriages, with Paris Metro trains later using rubber tyres and steel wheels. RAILWAY MAGAZINE ARCHIVE

ABOVE: Irish railways were at the forefront of diesel railcar development, for both 3ft and 5ft 3in gauge lines, particularly in the north and west of the island. In Northern Ireland, the LMS Northern Counties Committee (NCC) railcars Nos. 1-4 of 1933-38 were a great influence on the development of British railways railcars through to the 1950s. RAILWAY MAGAZINE ARCHIVE

ABOVE: The first diesel vehicles delivered to BR were 11 4w railbus cars built by Park Royal/BUT in 1954-57 and nicknamed the 'Flying Bricks'. Used by the London Midland Region, they had all been withdrawn by the end of 1959 after the introduction of new BR DMUs. RAIL PHOTOPRINTS

Leyland 125hp diesel engines drove the inner axle of each bogie. With six engines, the train could deliver 750hp and a maximum speed of 75mph.

It worked successfully on the LMS cross-country route between Oxford and Cambridge and later between Nottingham and St Pancras before going into store when the Second World War started in 1939. Unfortunately it never worked again, although the engine and transmission arrangement was a direct influence on later BR railcars built at Derby.

Irish Pioneers

Of all the railways in the British Isles, Ireland's rural narrow gauge lines probably faced the greatest struggle to survive. Serving depopulated districts on the fringes of the island, companies such as the County Donegal Joint Railway Co. (CDJRC) were constantly facing the threat of closure.

In 1910, the CDJRC appointed Henry Forbes as General Manager and over the next 33 years he made the 3ft gauge railway a pioneer of diesel traction for lightly trafficked lines. Railcar No. 1 was built in 1906 as an open inspection car, but fitted with an enclosed body in 1920, paving the way for larger diesel railcars introduced over the following three decades.

The CDJRC's first purpose-built diesel railcar was built in 1930 – the first to be introduced in the British Isles – followed by two petrol-engined cars delivered before the railway moved to diesels as their standard traction for passenger services in 1934. Eight further articulated railcars were built by Walker Bros. of Wigan between 1934 and 1951, transforming passenger services on the 106-mile network. Ultimately though, the railcars couldn't prevent the demise of the Donegal network, which closed in 1960.

Henry Forbes was also a member of the management committee for the rural Clogher Valley Railway, and persuaded the railway to purchase two notable diesel vehicles in 1932/33. A 28-seat passenger railcar was delivered first, followed by a unique rail lorry in 1933. Both vehicles moved to the CDJRC after the CVR closed at the end of 1941.

Encouraged by the potential of the narrow gauge diesels, the LMS-owned Northern Counties Committee (NCC) introduced four 5ft 3in gauge diesel railcars between 1933 and 1938. These vehicles, with their lightweight construction, underfloor Leyland engines and hydraulic transmission were the forerunners of the GWR diesel railcars and almost every British DMU and railcar since can trace its origins to the NCC pioneers. Nos. 1-4 were able to haul trailers and vans and run at up to 60mph, greatly increasing their flexibility and potential for use on main line, as well as branch line, services.

Several other Irish railways were quick to see the potential of diesel railcars and railbuses in the 1930s and 1940s. The Great Northern Railway (Ireland) and Sligo, Leitrim & Northern Counties Railway used a combination of converted road buses and railcars to work lightly-used lines until the late-1950s, while the GNR(I) also bought some superb AEC railcars for main line express work in 1950.

Railcar Evolution

Back on the British side of the Irish Sea, the GWR's AEC railcars are the best-known of the early diesel-engined vehicles. Taking their influences from the bus and lorry industry, they used standard diesel engines, bus type chassis and mechanical transmission.

Introduced in 1934, the prototype No. 1 was built by Park Royal and had a 130hp AEC underfloor engine, 69 seats and a streamlined body. It was joined by three similar railcars, fitted with buffet counters, for long-distance main line work (Nos. 2-4) in the same year.

Between 1935 and 1942 a further 33 AEC railcars were built for the GWR by Gloucester RCW and Swindon Works, including standard cars for branch line services, two parcels cars and four 'power twin' sets which could work with passenger coaches as intermediate trailers. These vehicles were the first to demonstrate the wider potential of diesel railcars for main line use, and alongside other experimental railcars played a direct role in the development of BR's DMU fleet, which started to appear in the mid-1950s.

Flying Bricks

The Second World War, its aftermath and Nationalisation of the 'Big Four' railways in 1948 created a hiatus in the development of new technologies for some years, but British Railways' thoughts soon turned to diesel railcars again. On January 1, 1948 the newly-created BR owned just 37 diesel railcar vehicles, 35 of which were absorbed from the GWR.

The first new post-war diesel prototype was a set of three 4w railbuses built by Park Royal and AEC in 1954. Nicknamed the 'Flying Bricks', the three-car train was formed of two Driving Motor cars and an intermediate trailer. Initially they were Nos. 1-3, but later given the BR numbers M79740-742. Tested in various locations, they had settled on the LMR by January 1955. A further three-car set and spare motor and trailer car (M79743-750) were delivered in 1955 and another three-car in 1957.

They worked on the Watford Junction-St Albans Abbey and Harrow-Belmont branches, but were not well regarded and all were withdrawn in February 1959 and scrapped by the end of 1963.

Around the same time, the lightweight 4w railbus concept was being tested again when BR ordered 22 vehicles from five different suppliers. Park Royal, Bristol/Eastern Coachworks, Wickham, AC Cars and Germany's Waggon und Maschinenbau built the railbuses in 1958/59 to work threatened branch lines in East Anglia,

Extreme Railcar Propulsion

While British and Irish railways saw railcars as a way to operate lines more economically, elsewhere in the world lightweight railcars were used for high-speed trials. The German *Schienenzeppelin* was an experimental railcar designed and developed by aircraft engineer Franz Kruckenberg in 1929. It used an aircraft engine and two-bladed propeller at the rear of the vehicle, which on June 21, 1931 pushed the railcar to a remarkable 143mph on the Hamburg-Berlin main line. This speed was not beaten on rails until 1954 and remains a record for a petrol-driven rail vehicle. However, due to safety concerns (not to mention its numerous other impracticalities) it was sidelined and dismantled in 1939.

As with aircraft, jet technology replaced propellers after the Second World War and two extraordinary railcars were built in the Soviet Union and the USA in the 1960s/70s.

In 1966, the New York Central Railroad fitted two turbojet engines to Budd RDC railcar M-497 which took the vehicle to a maximum of 184mph. Meanwhile in the USSR, the SVL high-speed laboratory (pictured) railcar similarly saw two jet engines installed on the roof of an ER22 EMU driving car in 1970, achieving a maximum of 160mph on test. The vehicle still exists in a derelict state in Russia but did not lead to any further examples, perhaps due to the noise and enormous fuel consumption of jet engines for railway operation! ●

ABOVE: SVL high-speed laboratory railcar. ROBERT HUMM COLLECTION

ABOVE: The German *Schienenzeppelin*. ROBERT HUMM COLLECTION

the south Midlands and Scotland. Again though, they were not a success and all had gone by 1967/68, along with the lines they were built to work.

Although the railbuses did not have the desired impact, the mass introduction of diesel railcars by BR in the 1950s and early-1960s transformed the operation of many lines and expanded to include cross-country and even inter-city services.

Today, the diesel multiple unit (DMU) is the dominant train type away from the electrified network of the UK's biggest cities, with designs encompassing everything from four-wheel 'Pacer' railbuses to 125mph 'Voyagers' and even the new Hitachi bi-mode Intercity Express Trains. Every one of these trains with underfloor diesel engines can trace its origins back to those pioneering railcars of the early 20th century. ●

Diesel Makes its Mark

As internal combustion engine technology developed, the potential for larger and more powerful locomotives grew and they eventually attracted the attention of the main line operators all over the world.

ABOVE: In March 1937 three experimental LMS shunting locomotives line up for the camera at Crewe South shed. On the left is the unique Sentinel-Doble 4w vertical boiler prototype, centre stage is English Electric 0-6-0DE No. 7078, forerunner of the LMS and BR standard 350hp shunters, while to the right is one of the larger 0-6-0DEs with jackshaft drive. RAIL PHOTOPRINTS

As events such as the global economic depression of the 1930s and the steady growth of competition from road transport ate into the dominance of railway companies, they inevitably looked for ways to save costs and find more efficient ways of working.

The success of the early diesel and petrol railcars in Ireland and elsewhere did not go unnoticed and as engine technology improved, the potential of larger locomotives for heavier work became apparent.

As well as saving staff costs by eliminating the fireman, diesel shunters offered the potential for working almost 24 hours a day, whereas small steam locomotives needed to stop much more regularly for water, coal and servicing.

Although the principles of internal combustion had been known since around 200BC, and various inventors had experimented with piston engines since the 17th century, it was not until the late-19th century that engineers such as Gottlieb Daimler and Rudolph Diesel created successful lightweight, fast-running and powerful engines running on petroleum, kerosene or, in Diesel's case, heavier fuel oil.

The world's first oil-engined railway locomotive was built by Priestman Brothers of Hull in 1894. This small four-wheel standard gauge vehicle had a vertically mounted twin-cylinder 12hp marine type engine driving the wheels via a crankshaft and large flywheel. It was tested by the Hull & Barnsley Railway, shunting wagons at Hull's Alexandra Dock although it was limited to hauling just one wagon at a time.

Over the next two decades, oil-engined locomotives were limited to small industrial and narrow gauge types due to their low power. Richard Hornsby & Sons of Grantham built the first commercially successful locomotives – six were built for military use between 1896 and 1903 and worked at Woolwich Arsenal ammunitions factory. Other early petrol/diesel locomotives were built by Maudslay of Coventry, F.C. Blake of Kew, Wolseley Tool & Motor Co., Kerr Stuart, McEwan Pratt, The Drewry Car Co. and miniature steam locomotive builder W.J. Bassett-Lowke, all before 1910.

Over the next two decades, as internal combustion engine technology improved, the locomotives steadily increased in size and power. Their development was accelerated by the necessities of the First World War, which introduced petrol and diesel vehicles to the battlefield, including the famous Simplex field railway locomotives. Throughout the 1920s, many experimental machines were proposed and built, although they remained relatively small and low-powered by modern standards. However, they proved useful for narrow

gauge, industrial and export applications.

Elsewhere in the world, companies such as MAN, Krupp and Maybach in Germany, Sulzer of Switzerland and Frichs in Denmark were developing diesel engines in the 400hp-1,200hp range and well as smaller, lower-powered engines for shunters and railcars.

By 1932 the Diesel Traction Department of Armstrong-Whitworth in Newcastle upon Tyne had constructed what could be considered the joint precursor (with English Electric demonstrator No. 7079 of 1936) of a vast fleet of 0-6-0 diesel-electric shunters for British Railways. A-W started building Sulzer and Saurer engines under licence in 1931 and bought in electrical equipment from the likes of English Electric, Crompton-Parkinson and Brown-Boveri.

The demonstrator, works number D8, entered service in July 1932 and was fitted with the same traction equipment used in the experimental Armstrong-Whitworth diesel railcars. It spent much of 1932/33 working in LNER goods yards in the Newcastle area. Trials included taking 800 ton loads up the 1-in-150 Benton Bank.

However, despite its capabilities, the LNER showed no interest at the time, and after a brief period with the Southern Railway it was obtained by Preston Corporation for use at Ribble Dock. This important link in the British diesel locomotive story was finally withdrawn in the winter of 1968. The LMS bought ten similar locomotives from A-W in 1935-36.

Just as notable were three four-axle bogie diesel-electrics ordered by the Ford Motor Co. for shunting at its Dagenham plant, and delivered by British Thomson-Houston (BTH) in 1932. Built by Metropolitan-Vickers in Sheffield for BTH, they were among the very few bogie shunting locomotives ever built in Britain. Rated at just 150hp, they combined an Allen six-cylinder in-line diesel with BTH electrical equipment and were designed for arduous shunting work in the plant's steelworks – a job they performed until 1968. One of these important pioneers is now preserved at the Kent & East Sussex Railway.

Main Line Breakthough

The London Midland & Scottish Railway (LMS) pioneered the use of diesel locomotives for shunting work in the UK, testing a variety of experimental and production machines from several suppliers. However, its first experimental diesel shunter was a remarkable 1932 Derby Works rebuild of former Midland Railway '1F' 0-6-0T No. 1831.

The boxy diesel retained the number of the original 1892-built locomotive but very little else, although below the body it closely resembled a steam locomotive, using the frames and driving wheels of the '1F'.

Powered by a Davey-Paxman six-cylinder engine of 400hp (later derated to 300hp), it employed a Haslam & Newton hydraulic transmission and had a small driving cab at each end.

No. 1831 was not regarded as very successful, but it provided useful experience for the further development of diesel shunter designs. It was stored in 1936, withdrawn in September 1939 and converted to a mobile power unit, emerging in its new guise as MPU3 in November 1940. It was withdrawn again in August 1951 and finally scrapped at Crewe Works sometime after September 1955.

A further nine prototype diesel shunters were procured by the LMS from various suppliers in the mid-1930s to compare different types of transmission and power units.

No. 7400 (quickly renumbered No. 7050) was a small 0-4-0 diesel-mechanical built in 1934 by The Drewry Car Co. at the English Electric Dick, Kerr works in Preston. Designed for light shunting in goods yards and docks, it weighed just 25 tons and had a 160hp W.H. Allen engine (later replaced by a Gardner unit). It was capable of 12mph, but its 7ft wheelbase allowed it to work over tightly-curved lines alongside locomotives such as the famous Lancashire & Yorkshire Railway 'Pugs'.

No. 7050 lived an interesting life, working in Salford until 1940 when it was loaned to the Air Ministry and eventually sold to the War Department (WD) in March 1943. It continued to work for the Army and the Royal Navy at various locations until it was preserved at the Museum of Army Transport in Beverley in 1979. When that museum closed it transferred to the National Collection and now resides at the National Railway Museum in York.

Made in Leeds

LMS No. 7401/7051 was built in 1932 as a demonstrator by Hunslet of Leeds but was tested and subsequently purchased by the LMS in May 1933. Like No. 7050, it was loaned to the WD in 1940, went back to the LMS in 1941-44, but returned to military duty as WD No. 27/70027 in August 1944. It was withdrawn by the LMS in December 1945 and sold back to Hunslet.

A small 0-6-0 diesel-mechanical, No. 7051 originally had an MAN six-cylinder engine rated at 150hp, although this was later replaced with a McLaren-Ricardo ML6 of 132hp.

After periods as a works shunter and a hire locomotive it was preserved at the Middleton Railway in its home city in September 1960 and remains there today as a cherished part of the railway's fleet.

LMS Nos. 7402/7052, 7053 and 7054 were also Hunslet 0-6-0DMs built in 1934 but fitted with McLaren-Benz, Brotherhood-Ricardo and Davey-Paxman engines respectively.

No. 7402 also went on loan to the WD in 1940 before being sold in December 1943 and flameproofed for use at RNAD Broughton Moor in Cumberland. It continued in military use until 1966, after which it spent three years working for a scrap metal yard at Long Marston in Warwickshire before being scrapped.

No. 7053 was less fortunate, going on loan to the WD between 1939 and 1942, but sold back to Hunslet in December 1942 and seeing no further use before being scrapped in the mid-1950s.

Meanwhile, No. 7054 was taken into LMS in November 1934, and also worked for the WD between 1939 and 1942 before being sold and renumbered WD No. 225 in May 1943.

In 1947, it was sold to Hunslet, where it was stored for seven years before being hired to, and later bought by, the National Coal Board. It was rebuilt with a Rolls-Royce engine in 1960–61 and worked at a number of collieries before being withdrawn and scrapped in 1974.

Nos. 7055/56 were also built in Leeds, by Hudswell Clarke, in 1934 and were 0-6-0DMs powered by Mirrlees-Ricardo eight-cylinder diesel engines. They were withdrawn in April/May 1939 and converted to Mobile Power Units – MPU2 and MPU1 respectively

– in May 1940/October 1940. They were scrapped in February 1964/January 1965.

Belfast Child

Perhaps the most unusual supplier of the early diesel shunters was Belfast shipbuilder Harland & Wolff, which built LMS No. 7057 in 1934. An 0-6-0DM with an H&W/Burmeister & Wain 'Harlandic' 175hp three-cylinder engine, was tested from July 1934 and accepted into LMS stock in February 1935, loaned to the WD in 1941-43 and sold back to H&W in January 1944. On its return to Belfast it was rebuilt with a 225hp engine and converted to 5ft 3in Irish standard gauge and sold to the LMS Northern Counties Committee. As NCC No. 22 it survived until 1965, when it was withdrawn and scrapped.

No. 7408/7058 started life in 1932 as an Armstrong-Whitworth 0-6-0 diesel-electric prototype. It was tested by the LMS and taken into stock in February 1934. Fitted with an Armstrong-Sulzer 250hp six-cylinder engine it weighed 40 tons and featured a jackshaft drive arrangement. The electric transmission, greater power and heavier weight made it the precursor of thousands of LMS and BR 0-6-0DEs, some of which are still working today. In contrast to the steam locomotives ▶

ABOVE: LMS No. 1831 was the company's first diesel shunter, built on the frames of a Midland '1F' 0-6-0T in 1932. This view, thought to be at Crewe Works, clearly shows the locomotive's steam origins. COLOUR-RAIL

ABOVE: English Electric-built Nos. 7069-78 were the first 0-6-0DEs to use the EE 6K 350hp engine and two axle-hung traction motors, which was to become the standard configuration for most large diesel shunters built in the UK and for export. The ten LMS locomotives were joined by an EE demonstrator which became No. 7079. COLOUR-RAIL

ABOVE: LMS Nos. 7080-7119 were two batches of 20 single motor, jackshaft drive 350hp 0-6-0DEs built by EE between May 1939 and July 1942. Nos. 7100–7109 were loaned to the WD in 1941, with some remaining in Egypt and Italy after the war. The remaining 30 became BR Nos. 12003–032, with all but one remaining in traffic until 1966/67. COLOUR-RAIL

ABOVE: The LNER showed comparatively little interest in diesel shunters, but did order its own prototype 0-6-0DE in 1941. No. 8000 was built at Doncaster Works in 1944-45, using components supplied by English Electric and was later joined by four more locomotives, later classified Diesel Electric Shunting 1 (DES1) for the four EE machines and DES2 for the lone Brush example. COLOUR-RAIL

it was designed to replace, it carried enough fuel for a week's shunting work.

It was loaned to the WD in 1941-1943 and used at the famous Longmoor Military Railway. Although it passed into BR ownership in 1948 it was withdrawn in November 1949 before its new number (No. 13000) could be applied.

Production Builds

The early prototypes quickly proved that diesel traction could deliver much greater efficiency for shunting duties and the LMS placed orders for more 0-6-0DEs in the mid- to late-1930s.

Nos. 7059-68 were similar to No. 7058, but fitted with a more powerful 350hp Armstrong-Sulzer engine and a single Crompton-Parkinson traction motor attached to double reduction gears and the jackshaft drive. Delivered to Crewe South (Nos. 7059-63) and Carlisle Kingmoor (Nos. 7064-68) in 1936, they were requisitioned by the WD in 1940/41 and later in the Second World War eight were sent to France, Belgium, the Netherlands and Egypt. After hostilities ceased they remained scattered across the four countries, with Nos. 7059/61/64/67 working for Belgian Railways until the 1960s and four seeing use with Egyptian Railways. Nos. 7062/63 remained in the UK but although No. 7063 survived in industrial use until 1966 none were preserved.

English Electric's Nos. 7069-79 were the first 0-6-0DEs to use the EE 6K 350hp engine and two axle-hung traction motors, which was to become the standard configuration for most large diesel shunters built in the UK and for export to several other countries.

Ten LMS locomotives plus an EE demonstrator which became No. 7079 were built. Nos. 7074/76/79 stayed with the LMS and later became BR Nos. 12000-002, while the others were sold to the WD in 1940 and shipped to France. Remarkably, No. 7069 survived the war and went into industrial use in France. It was repatriated in 1988 and is currently being restored at the Vale of Berkeley Railway in Gloucestershire.

By now, the LMS shunters were starting to take on a look that will be

familiar to modern eyes. Nos. 7080-7119 were two batches of 20 single motor, jackshaft drive 350hp 0-6-0DEs built by EE between May 1939 and July 1942.

Some of the first 20 were put to work shunting the huge hump yard at Toton, near Nottingham, by mid-1939. An order for a further 20 units was placed in 1939. Nos. 7100–7109 were loaned to the WD in 1941, and sold the following year. All ten survived the war with six being sold to Egyptian Railways and four to Italian State Railways where they became Class Ne.700. The remaining 30 became BR Nos. 12003–032, with all but one remaining in traffic until 1966/67.

The final LMS design was the direct predecessor of BR's standard large diesel shunter. Nos. 7120-29 were built in 1945 and construction eventually ran to 120 examples under BR ownership. Externally very similar to the later Class 08s, the LMS/BR Class 11s were withdrawn in 1967-72 but many continued in industrial use with the NCB and ICI and some survive in preservation.

Almost 100 near-identical locomotives were sold to Netherlands Railways by EE between 1950 and 1957, with 21 others going to Australia. Some of the Dutch locomotives are still earning their keep on the main line in 2017, while others have been repatriated and preserved by British heritage railways.

LNER trials

Several years after the LMS trials commenced, the LNER ordered its own prototype 0-6-0DE in 1941. Built at Doncaster Works in 1944-45, using components supplied by English Electric, the four 'J45' locomotives, later classified Diesel Electric Shunting 1, (DES1s) were similar to LMS Nos. 7069-79, Southern Railway Nos. 1-3 and GWR No. 2 (see below).

A fifth locomotive was added in 1945, but with Brush diesel-electric components rated at 360hp, and classified DES2. The four DES1s became Nos. 15000-003 between 1950 and 1952. They spent most of their careers shunting at Whitemoor Yard near March and all four were withdrawn by 1967.

The lone DES2 was completed by November 1947 and allocated LNER No.

8004, although it never carried this number. It became BR No. 15004 in May 1949 and worked at various locations, including Stratford and Whitemoor. It also worked at Woodford Halse and New England in Peterborough before being withdrawn in 1962.

GWR & Southern

Although it was an enthusiastic and early adopter of diesel traction for passenger railcars, the GWR only acquired two diesel shunters before Nationalisation in 1948.

No. 1 was a standard Fowler 0-4-0 70hp diesel-mechanical design built in 1933 and used at Swindon Works until 1940, when it was sold to the Ministry of Supply.

No. 2 was a considerably larger 0-6-0DE, built by Hawthorn Leslie in 1936 and similar in appearance to LMS Nos. 7069-79 and Southern Railway diesels Nos. 1-3. It became BR No. 15100 in 1948, was withdrawn in 1965 and scrapped in early-1966. A further seven diesel shunters were ordered by the GWR before Nationalisation, but not delivered until 1948/49. No. 501 (BR No. 15107) was a Brush-Petter 360hp 0-6-0DE, while Nos. 502-507 (BR Nos. 15101-106) were English Electric machines. The six EE machines were initially based at Old Oak Common for use in Acton Yard before moving to South Wales for shunting at Cardiff East Dock until August 1967. No. 15107 had a shorter life, being delivered to Bristol in 1949 and withdrawn at Swindon Works in June 1958.

A much smaller user of shunting locomotives than the other three 'Big Four' companies, the Southern nevertheless obtained a trio of EE/Hawthorn Leslie 350hp 0-6-0DE prototypes. Under Richard Maunsell's direction, bodies for Nos. 1-3 were built in 1937 at Ashford Works but fitted out by EE in Preston. Loaned to the WD in 1941-45, they became BR Nos. 15201-203 and worked at Norwood Junction in south London until November/December 1964.

The legacy of these early machines can still be seen on the British rail network today in the form of scores of surviving Class 08s and 09s still earning their keep, providing unfussy, reliable and dependable service at depots, yards and preserved railways. ●

ABOVE: From February 1948 No. 10000 was placed on a twice-daily London-Derby diagram, hauling trains of 300t to 450t. No. 10001 also entered service on the London-Derby route when completed that year, running a regular **Derby-Manchester diagram.** ED BRUTON/RAILWAY MAGAZINE ARCHIVE

Main Line Diesel Pioneers

LMS 'Twins' Nos. 10000/01 are the most famous of the early diesels, but they weren't the first large locomotives to work on the British main line.

By the 1940s, the internal combustion engine was proving its worth in railway applications across the world. In North America, the flexibility and lower operating cost of diesel traction was eagerly adopted by railroads under attack from road haulage, the private car and air travel, but in Britain, diesel traction was limited to a few demonstrators and a fleet of shunters introduced by the LMS, as we've seen. Newcastle engineering giant Armstrong Whitworth in particular was promoting the use of diesel traction for railways.

A-W was famous around the world for its industrial and manufacturing prowess. Involved in many areas that were, for the

time, cutting edge technology, the company forged its reputation manufacturing armaments, railway locomotives (including many of the LMS 'Black Fives'), aircraft and motor cars, as well as machinery, mechanical and electrical equipment, cranes, bridges and shipbuilding.

Although it largely built steam locomotives for export, A-W obtained a licence to build diesel engines from the Swiss firm Sulzer in 1919 and by the early-1930s was experimenting with diesel traction for railway use.

In 1933 it completed a 1-Co-1 diesel-electric locomotive as a speculative venture and sent it for trials on the London & North Eastern Railway

(LNER). Designed as a mixed traffic, main line machine, as opposed to the small shunters that it had previously built (see page 56), the locomotive had a top speed of 70mph, maximum axle loading of 17 tons and a maximum starting tractive effort of 28,500lb.

As a foretaste of things to come, it was also fitted with multiple working equipment to enable a pair of locomotives to be controlled by a single driver hauling goods trains of up to 1,500t or 500t passenger trains at up to 60mph on level track. Working alone, it could haul an 800t goods train or a 260t passenger train.

The six driving wheels had a diameter of 4ft and Iso-thermos axleboxes with an

ABOVE: Official works portrait of Britain's first main line diesel, Armstrong-Whitworth D9. This 800hp 1-Co-1 was capable of 70mph and was extensively tested by the LNER in north-east England in 1934. It was withdrawn after an engine failure and dismantled in 1937. RAILWAY MAGAZINE ARCHIVE

equalised spring arrangement. Sanding was provided on the outer driving wheels with air supplied from a small compressor. Automatic vacuum brakes were provided for hauling passenger and fitted goods trains.

An Armstrong-Sulzer 8LD28 eight-cylinder power unit, producing 800hp at 700rpm, was installed, attached to a main generator, and the diesel-generator set was supported directly by the locomotive's frame. A separate 80hp Armstrong-Saurer auxiliary engine was housed in the nose end, avoiding the need for a large and heavy set of batteries to start the main engine.

Unusually, the main engine had no metal rocker covers; instead roll-back leather covers were used, held in place by spring fasteners. Two side-mounted radiators provided cooling for the water and lubricating oil, air being drawn through by a roof mounted scavenger

fan, an arrangement that would shape the design of BR diesels 25 years later. The fuel tanks and batteries were positioned either side of the main power unit. Full output of the diesel engine was available from 6mph to 65mph. Three Crompton Parkinson axle-hung traction motors powered the driving axles.

The demonstrator made its first outing on LNER metals on July 6, 1933, working between Newcastle and Alnmouth and between Newcastle and Hexham. Further tests in 1933/34 included hauling goods trains of 45 and 60 wagons between Newcastle and Berwick and south over the East Coast Main Line to York and passenger trains on the Newcastle-Carlisle line. Unfortunately the LNER showed little interest, and a crankcase explosion in June 1934 led to its retirement after running around 26,000 miles. It

was stored at A-W's Scotswood works until 1937 when it was dismantled.

However, while there was still much resistance from steam-minded engineers and other vested interests, a few senior railway engineers were gradually being persuaded of efficiency of diesels over their steam equivalents. Having invested in diesel shunters, the LMS started to investigate the use of diesel locomotives for main line work before the Second World War. Around the same time, the Southern Railway was considering diesel traction for lines where electrification could not be justified.

Non-identical twins

The London Midland & Scottish Railway discovered the benefits of diesel traction as early as 1927 and during the 1930s acquired a diverse fleet of shunting ▶

ABOVE: Resplendent in gloss black, Nos. 10000/01 pass Weaver Junction on the West Coast Main Line with an express in 1949. They could be used singly as a mixed traffic '5MT' equivalent or together as a 3,200hp unit for hauling heavy express passenger trains. RAIL PHOTOPRINTS

ABOVE: In spring 1953, 10000/01 were transferred to the Southern Region, for comparison with 1-Co-Co-1 prototypes 10201/202. Here they saw use on Western Section passenger duties, predominantly on the Bournemouth route hauling trains such as 'The Royal Wessex'. COLOUR-RAIL

locomotives. Development was stalled by the Second World War, but in 1946 the company authorised the construction of two 1,600hp prototypes for main line duties. While they were not the first British main line diesel, that honour fell to Armstrong-Whitworth's demonstrator of 1933 (see page 40), they were the first to be ordered and built by a main line company and the vanguard of a new generation of railway traction.

Built in just six months, No. 10000 was unveiled on December 5, 1947, less than four weeks before the LMS was nationalised. It was followed in July 1948 by its non-identical twin – No. 10001. Both were built at Derby Works, using English Electric diesel engines and electrical equipment.

The pair were initially based at Camden shed in north London and used mainly for their first few years (except for a brief period on the Midland Main Line in 1948/49) on West Coast Main Line passenger duties. The locomotives were assessed both singly and in multiple against ex-LMS 'Pacifics' on express trains such as 'The Royal Scot', but also worked lesser trains and goods. Two additional 'Princess Coronation' 4-6-2s, Nos. 46256/257, were built to a modified H.G. Ivatt design for direct comparison with the new form of traction.

At 1,600hp, they were designed as mixed traffic locomotives, capable of working singly to replace locomotives such as LMS Stanier/Fowler '4P' 2-6-4Ts on secondary and outer suburban work, 'Black Five' 4-6-0s on fast freight and secondary passenger or '5XP' 4-6-0s on lighter expresses. Used in pairs, they were a match for the company's

'Pacifics' on crack expresses, maintaining fast schedules with heavy trains.

From February 1948 No. 10000 was placed on a twice-daily London-Derby (128.5 mile) return diagram, hauling trains of 300 to 450 gross tons. No. 10001 also entered service on the London-Derby route when completed, running a regular Derby-Manchester diagram.

In late-1948 both machines were withdrawn for modifications based on service experience. They returned to Midland Main Line duty, before switching

to work Euston-Carlisle-Glasgow expresses in multiple. On June 1, 1949 they operated the 16-carriage, 545t 'Royal Scot' non-stop from Euston to Glasgow, returning south the following day. On the climbs to Shap and Beattock the 'twins' operated at full power, cresting the summits unaided at 38mph and 36mph respectively. From June 1949 they worked in multiple for more than two months on London-Carlisle and London-Glasgow trains.

From mid-1949 the pair were separated, with No.10000 deployed

ABOVE: In July 1948, the 'Twins' grab the attention of permanent way gangers as they arrive at Preston with an Up express for London Euston. The immaculate black and silver machines must have seemed like something from the future compared to the many elderly steam locomotives that were still around at the time. RAILWAY MAGAZINE ARCHIVE

on the Euston-Blackpool route, and No.10001 operating London-Glasgow trains. Other work included London-Crewe and Liverpool. On the 'Red Rose' express No. 10001 recorded 82mph on a down gradient with a load of 490 tons.

They were also used on express goods trains including Camden-Crewe and Crewe-Willesden; the locomotives met the scheduled average speed of 45mph on Camden-Crewe trains with 500t trains. One notable working was the haulage of a 60 wagon, 1,100t coal train between Rugby and Willesden, maintaining 25mph on a 1-in-133 gradient to Tring.

Other outings included a trial on the Settle-Carlisle line, workings to Perth and, on one occasion, to Aberdeen – the furthest north they ever worked. Unreliable steam heating boilers meant that they were used on goods traffic during the winter and passenger trains in the summer when heating was less important.

In spring 1953, 10000/01 were transferred to the Southern Region, for comparison with 1-Co-Co-1 prototypes 10201/202 and later 10203 (see page 50). Here they saw use on Western Section passenger duties, predominantly on the Bournemouth route. By mid-1955, all five diesels were allocated to the LMR, where they took turns on WCML expresses and later Euston-Bletchley outer-suburban services.

A number of small modifications were made to the 'twins' during their career: 10000 received extra strengthening ribs on the bogie sideframes, matching those fitted to its sister from new, and had the boiler fuel and water tank filler access panels (located on the body side, just below cantrail level) filled in; both of these alterations being made in September 1948. Eight months later, the

same machine also had the two small areas of valance, immediately inboard of each buffer, removed to permit a more convenient fitting of multiple working jumper sockets. Again, this brought the earlier locomotive in line with 10001.

Both locomotives entered works in early 1953 to have extra lamp brackets fitted to each end, prior to running on the Southern Region. Small, flush-fitting electric light apertures were also added adjacent to each bracket. The SR power classification of 6P/5F was applied, differing from the 5P/5F of the LM Region. Following their sojourn 'down south', the extra brackets were removed (in 1956), although all of the electric lights remained until withdrawal.

The water scoop equipment saw modification, the main visible difference being the addition of a raised roof panel on either side of the boiler compartment as well as flat-section trunking between the battery box and bogie at the No.2 end. This modification was made to 10000 late in 1955, while 10001 was not dealt with until October 1957.

One of the final modifications, in 1961, was the adding of a set of small grab handles, fixed to the waist strip on each corner of the nose, along with a pair of similar handles on the nose doors, just above the waist. Only 10001 received these extra adornments, although both sported overhead electrification warning symbols and red diamond coupling codes from 1960.

Until 1951, 10000 carried raised LMS lettering on its bodyside, but 10001 – completed in July 1948 – did not. From 1951, both locomotives carried the early BR emblem. In early 1956, the original black livery with silver trim was replaced by BR Brunswick green with steam style orange-black-orange lining and 'primrose yellow' roof panels.

Deliveries of new BR diesels gradually reduced the need for the two prototypes and their use diminished until 10000 was withdrawn and stored at Derby Works in 1963. As the last to be overhauled, 10001 worked on until March 1966, surviving long enough to receive small yellow warning panels on the nose ends. After a lengthy period in store, these British diesel pioneers were finally sold for scrap in 1968. Had they survived for another couple of years there's a good chance someone would have recognised their importance and saved one or both of these pioneering machines. As it is, the scrapman denied us the chance to preserve locomotives that paved the way for several generations of British Railways diesels, and a number of export designs for Africa, Australia and elsewhere.

December 2017 marks the 70th anniversary of the unveiling of No. 10000 at Derby. Much has been written about these two pioneering locomotives – both positive and negative – but at this distance the evidence points to a remarkably successful experiment in diesel traction. Despite the many difficulties they faced operating on a railway set up for steam locomotives, not to mention issues such as crewing, maintenance and repairs, they provided a tremendous amount of valuable experience for BR in this field.

Development work carried out by BR and EE on these two locomotives led to successful production designs including Classes 37 and 40, DP2 and Class 50, while the bogie design was used, virtually unaltered, for the 'EM2' Co-Co electrics built for the Woodhead route. Descendants of their successful power units were used in the 3,300hp Class 56 and Class 58 of the 1970s and 1980s, and continue to provide sterling service today in many surviving EE diesels. ●

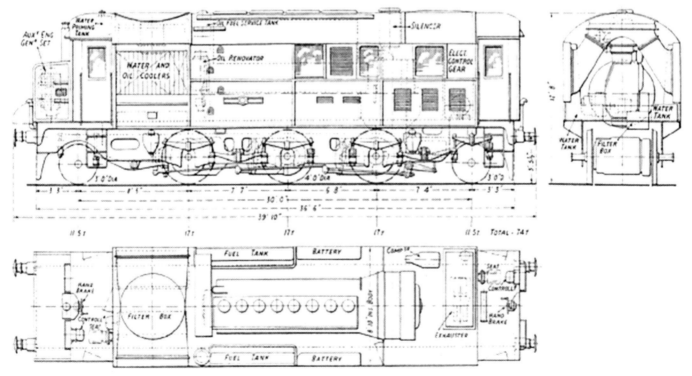

ABOVE: General arrangement drawing of the Armstrong-Whitworth 1-Co-1 diesel. RAILWAY MAGAZINE ARCHIVE

ABOVE: This view of No. 10202 at Brighton in July 1952 gives some sense of the steam-era environment into which the early prototype diesels were launched. Maintenance in filthy depots alongside steam locomotives made it difficult to keep the locomotives, their power units and electrical equipment in good order. RAIL PHOTOPRINTS

Southern Giants: 10201-203

Best known for his innovative steam locomotives, Southern Railway Chief Mechanical Engineer O.V.S. Bulleid was also involved in the development of diesel and electric traction, including a trio of large locomotives delivered after Nationalisation.

The two main line diesels commissioned by the Southern Railway actually pre-dated the LMS English Electric pioneers (page 64) by several years but due to leisurely construction they did not enter traffic until 1950. Thus the SR machines never really received the prominence which they deserved. A joint exercise by the SR Chief Mechanical Engineer, O.V.S. Bulleid and English Electric, they were distinctive

machines whose rounded body shape matched the Bulleid coaches which were coming on stream at the same time.

Despite their EE electrical and mechanical design the Southern's influence was evident in the flush cab front, devoid of English Electric's trademark 'noses.' The eight-wheel bogies, with outer carrying axles giving a 1-Co-Co-1 wheel arrangement to reduce the weight on each axle, were an innovation which would subsequently

appear on the early Type 4 diesel designs from both English Electric (Class 40) and BR Derby/Sulzer (Classes 44-46).

In all, the Southern Region built three locomotives, the first two (Nos. 10201/202) at Ashford in 1950 and the third (No. 10203) at Brighton in 1954. No. 10203 differed in some details and had its engine uprated to 2,000hp. It was the first diesel-electric of that power to run on BR and led directly to the development of the EE

Type 4 or Class 40. No. 10203 was also three tons lighter than its less powerful sisters. It was rated '7P/6F' under the power classification system adopted by BR, while the earlier locomotives were '6P/5F'.

By the time the first pair entered service, BR had settled on a striking black and silver livery for its diesels, and they wore this from new, unlike the earlier Bulleid/Raworth electric locomotives which carried SR malachite green in the late-1940s.

No. 10201 was run-in on the London Midland Region, working from St. Pancras, before going on show at the Festival of Britain in 1951 (pictured), from which it returned to traffic in September of that year.

No. 10202 was completed in August 1951 and sent to the SR's Western Section, based at Nine Elms shed in south London for Waterloo-Salisbury/Exeter duties. In 1952, both locomotives were on the Western Section, working expresses to Exeter and Bournemouth.

They worked the principal expresses including the 'Bournemouth Belle' and the 'Atlantic Coast Express' as far as Exeter. They were cleared to work as far as Plymouth but none ever did, although No. 10201 got as far as Exeter St David's when it, allegedly, ran away from Exeter Central. No. 10202 was also tested on the Eastern Section, working the 'Golden Arrow' and 'Night Ferry' Victoria-Dover boat trains early in 1954.

From March 1953 they were joined, for comparison purposes, by LMR Nos. 10000/001 on these diagrams. During 1955 all five pioneer diesels were transferred to the LMR, where Nos. 10201/202 were generally used as a pair, double-heading expresses such as 'The Royal Scot', like their LMR counterparts.

No. 10203 was delivered in 1954 and also tested on the 'Golden Arrow' and 'Night Ferry' in 1955.

During the same year, Nos. 10201/202 and 10000/001 moved back to the LMR, based at Willesden, followed later by No. 10203. While the 1,600hp locomotives

ABOVE: Representing the future of British Railways, No. 10201 was exhibited at the 1951 Festival of Britain site in Battersea with 'EM1' electric No. 26020, 'Britannia' 4-6-2 No. 70004 *William Shakespeare*, 'Fell' diesel No. 10100 and several other industrial and export locomotives. RAIL PHOTOPRINTS

ABOVE: In 1955 Nos. 10201/202 and 10000/001 moved to the LMR, based at Willesden, followed later by No. 10203. While the 1,600hp locomotives were used in pairs, their 2,000hp sister was considered powerful enough to handle such trains alone. In July 1958, it passes Winsford in Cheshire with the Euston-Glasgow 'Royal Scot'. RAIL PHOTOPRINTS

ABOVE: No. 10202 in the roundhouse at Willesden in the late-1950s. The communication doors fitted in the centre of the cab are prominent in this view. COLOUR-RAIL

ABOVE: No. 10203 was delivered in 1954 and tested on the 'Golden Arrow' and 'Night Ferry' in 1955. With the superb Pullman Car train in tow, the 2,000hp prototype passes Petts Wood, between Bromley and Orpington with the Dover-bound 'Arrow' in March 1955. COLOUR-RAIL

ABOVE: Just three months old and in original BR black with silver trim, No. 10202 stands among the ash and clinker at Nine Elms depot on November 3, 1951.

were used in pairs on WCML expresses, their 2,000hp sister was considered powerful enough to handle such trains alone. To facilitate crew access to both locomotives when working in multiple, Nos. 10201/202 were modified with communication doors between the windscreens and flexible gangways, although in practice they were rarely used.

As well as Anglo-Scottish trains, the locomotives also worked to Liverpool and Manchester, Euston-Bletchley outer-suburban trains and handled fitted goods trains on occasions.

During the mid-1950s the three

Southern machines were overhauled at Derby and repainted in BR green with the lower bodysides panelled in orange/black/orange lining, not unlike a steam locomotive tender. The later-style BR crest was applied and the roofs were painted primrose yellow!

As with many prototype locomotives, works visits were frequent and, usually, longer in duration than for production machines but Nos. 10201-203 were generally considered reliable.

Right at the end of its career, No. 10203 gained small yellow warning panels before withdrawal in 1962. Its older sisters did not receive the same treatment.

By 1960 there was little work for any of them and Nos. 10201/203 were withdrawn at the end of 1962, followed by No. 10202 the following spring. By this stage, BR had sufficient numbers of Pilot Scheme and production diesel locomotives and the non-standard trio, along with Nos. 10000/001, were surplus to requirements. Despite surviving until 1968, none of the Southern Region diesels was saved for posterity. However, experience gained during their trials was a direct influence on the first generation of BR diesels, including the first 2,000hp BR/EE 'Pilot Scheme' locomotives introduced in 1958. •

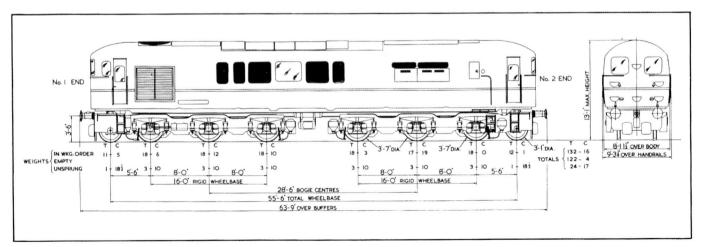

ABOVE: General arrangement drawing of the Southern 1-Co-Co-1 diesels. RAILWAY MAGAZINE ARCHIVE

SR 11001

Designed to handle both shunting and local trip work, this unique Bulleid diesel-mechanical proved less than adequate at both tasks and the experiment was not repeated.

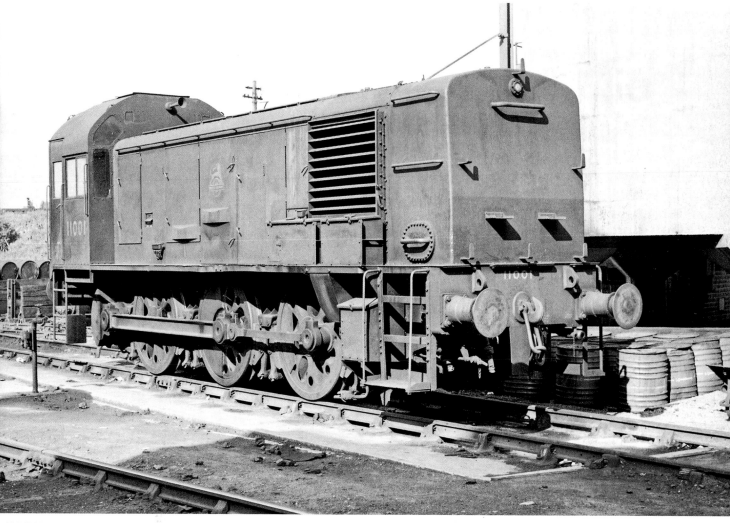

ABOVE: No. 11001 stabled between shunting duties at Norwood Yard in 1952. RAIL PHOTOPRINTS

Like Nos. 10201-203, this quirky 0-6-0 diesel-mechanical prototype had its origins with the Southern Railway but did not emerge until after Nationalisation. Completed in 1949 at Ashford Works, it was built to the design of O.V.S. Bulleid – the last SR Chief Mechanical Engineer and first CME of British Railways Southern Region. Construction started in 1947 but this one-off machine was not taken into BR stock until February 1950.

No. 11001 was powered by a Paxman Ricardo RPH Series 1 500hp engine powering a blind rear axle and crankshaft which drove the six wheels via coupling rods. A Vulcan Sinclair fluid coupling and sychro self-shifting (SSS) Powerflow gearbox provided three forward and reverse gears in either high or low range, with top speed ranging from 5mph first gear and low range up to a maximum of 36mph in third gear, high range.

Impressively, the tractive effort of 33,000lbf was the same as Bulleid's 'Q1' 0-6-0.

Interestingly, to overcome a lack of experience with driving diesel locomotives, Bulleid laid out the cab controls in the style of a steam locomotive. Another unusual feature was that the fuel tank was in the end of the long bonnet, normally where a radiator would be positioned on such a machine. No. 11001 also had that other Bulleid trademark feature – Bulleid-Firth-Brown 'Boxpok' cast wheels, in this instance of 4ft 6in diameter.

Unlike many of the early diesel shunting locomotives, which were intended purely for low speed yard work, No. 11001 was designed to be capable of both shunting and local trip freight work or branch line goods trains. Experience with the Maunsell and Bulleid 350hp 0-6-0DEs (see page 56) in the late-1930s showed that they were not fast or powerful enough for

trip working among the frequent electric suburban services around London.

Unfortunately, despite the logical attempt to design a machine capable of shunting and trip work, it proved inadequate at both. The low-speed range was reportedly too inflexible for shunting and the high speed range was too low for main line sorties.

Initially tested by the SR at Norwood Junction and Three Bridges yards, its only venture away from the region was a spell on loan at Stourton in Leeds in 1952, but soon fell out of use. It moved to Derby Works, at that time the national centre for diesel development, for repair but these were not completed until 1955. Originally painted plain black with the early BR emblem, it later carried BR green.

In 1956 it returned to the SR but was back in store at Ashford Works by 1959, withdrawn in August and scrapped in December of that year. ●

One Locomotive, Six Engines: The 'Fell' Diesel

This radical concept aimed to replicate the very flexible power supply of steam locomotives across the power range and create a 2,000hp locomotive at a time when powerful diesel engines were heavy and cumbersome.

ABOVE: Main line testing started on January 9, 1951 around Derby and later progressed to trials on St Pancras-Manchester express services. On March 20, 1952 No. 10100 passes Loughborough Midland with an Up express for London. RAIL PHOTOPRINTS

Probably the most unusual diesel locomotive ever to work for British Railways was the multi-engined, diesel-mechanical No. 10100, devised by Lt. Col. L.F.R. Fell, authorised by the LMS in 1947 and delivered in 1950. Fell had been an apprentice at Doncaster Works and an advocate of diesel power since the early-1930s.

No. 10100 was 2-D-2 (4-8-4) machine powered by four 500hp Davey Paxman RPHX V12 supercharged engines housed in the nose ends. These were coupled via a common gearbox to the two intermediate driving axles and each engine 'cut in' as speed increased. Two 150hp AEC engines were also installed for providing auxiliary power and air supply for the superchargers.

Two Laidlaw-Drew boilers were fitted for carriage heating, with feed water being pre-heated by the main engine exhausts. Boiler water supply could be replenished on the move via retractable pick-up gear and the water troughs situated along main lines of the time. Large Serck radiators were positioned at each nose end, cooling two main engines and one auxiliary engine each.

ABOVE: No. 10100 spent long periods out of service at Derby Works. On August 29, 1954 it was captured there undergoing attention. By this stage the middle section of the coupling rods had been removed. RAIL PHOTOPRINTS

ABOVE: One of the enormously complex spiral bevel gearboxes that were key to Lt. Col. Fell's multi-engine concept. ROBERT HUMM COLLECTION

ABOVE: A very sad looking No. 10100 in the Derby Works scrapyard with fellow prototype No. 10800 on April 21, 1960. RAILWAY MAGAZINE ARCHIVE

ABOVE: In recent years the multi-engine concept has returned with Bombardier offering its TRAXX diesel with four standard industrial engines that can be switched in and out as required to save fuel and even out wear-and-tear. Deutsche Bahn (DB) has almost 40 in service or on order; No. 245 015 stands at Munich Hbf in February 2015 with a train for Muhldorf. BEN JONES

The concept was far ahead of its time, and an attempt to replicate the very flexible power supply of steam locomotives across the power range, with constant power at the rail but with the greater efficiency of diesel traction. It also provided a method of constructing a 2,000hp locomotive at a time when single unit diesel engines of this power were much larger and heavier than they are today. Multiple engines also promised greater reliability and the ability to 'get home' in the event of an engine failure.

The four engines were engaged via a complex drive system using fluid couplings, pneumatic relays and dog clutches, using one engine at 0-6mph, two at 6-17mph, three for the 17-24mph range and four between 24mph and the top speed of 78mph.

Much like the MR's Paget 2-6-2, built 40 years earlier at Derby Works, the design was innovative with great potential, but the locomotive itself was something of an enigma.

Main line testing started on January 9, 1951 around Derby and later progressed to trials on St Pancras-Manchester express services. Its first test run to Manchester via the Peak Forest route ended with No. 10100 and the head of the train covered in a thick layer of soot, caused by the exhaust blast from the locomotive dislodging years of accumulated deposits from the lining of the many tunnels on the route!

Frequent visits were made to Derby Works for repair and modifications, including a long hiatus from August 1952 until at least September 1953. A major failure sidelined the locomotive for another year in 1954.

Repairs were eventually made, and No. 10100 was tested on the Settle-Carlisle line in 1955. On one outing it ran 18 miles from Appleby to Ais Gill summit in 25.25 minutes with 389 tons on the drawbar, achieving a power output of 1,900hp at 44mph. It then returned to the Midland Main Line and Derby-Manchester duties, although there were lengthy periods out of action at Derby Works. It was during one of these workings on October 16, 1958 that the locomotive was severely damaged by fire at Manchester Central, leading to its withdrawal and eventually scrapping in 1960. It was reportedly popular with drivers, being smooth starting and powerful and despite its complexity and advanced features it ran more than 100,000 miles in its eight-year life. However, it was less popular with fitters, being difficult to maintain and repair due to a lack of space in the engine rooms.

Like other early BR diesels, 10100 was painted black with silver trim from new. During a works visit in 1955, it gained BR green with a small early crest centrally positioned on the bodyside. By March 1957 it was in lined green with the later BR crest.

A number of modifications were made to 10100 during its brief career, but the most obvious was its alteration from 2-D-2 to 4-4-4-4 wheel arrangement in 1954. This involved the removal of the centre section of coupling rod on each side.

There is a comprehensive history of the locomotive in the RCTS book *LMS Diesel Locomotives and Railcars* by E.V. Richards (ISBN 0 901115 76 2).

Although the Fell concept was not adopted in the 1950s, the idea of multi-engined diesels has been resurrected very successfully in the 21st century. Bombardier's TRAXX family of modular locomotives includes a multi-engine diesel-electric that employs four heavy duty 540kW Caterpillar industrial engines. Sophisticated computer control replaces the complex mechanical linkages of the 'Fell', switching the engines in and out as required to save fuel and reduce emissions over traditional large single-engined diesel locomotives. Access panels in the bodyside allow quick replacement of any failed engines. Germany's Deutsche Bahn has almost 40 of the type in service or on order for regional and Intercity passenger work away from the electrified network. ●

First of the Type 1s: BR 10800

Forerunner of BR's Class 15 and 16s, this small mixed traffic diesel was inspired by North American 'hood' units and intended as a replacement for the LMS '4MT' 2-6-4T family.

ABOVE: In 1955 No. 10800 spent time working a Rugby-based 5MT 4-6-0 diagram between Rugby, Peterborough and Birmingham, hauling trains of up to ten bogies on particularly busy days. RAIL PHOTOPRINTS

For lighter mixed traffic duties on secondary and branch lines, replacing Stanier/Ivatt 2MT 2-6-2T steam locomotives, the London Midland & Scottish Railway worked with British Thompson-Houston (BTH) and the North British Locomotive Co. (NBL) to design and build a small four-axle diesel-electric locomotive. The companies devised a North American style 'hood' unit with a single cab positioned between a long bonnet containing the power unit and a shorter bonnet housing a steam heating boiler. Although designed by H.G. Ivatt for the LMS in 1945, the locomotive did not emerge until 1950, by which time the LMS had been absorbed by British Railways. The locomotive was built at NBL's Hyde Park factory in Glasgow and employed an 827hp Davey Paxman engine and BTH electrical equipment. The Paxman 16RPXHL turbocharged 16V diesel engine was linked to a BTH DC main generator delivering current to four axle-hung 155hp traction motors.

After initial testing in Scotland, including a trip from Glasgow to Ardrossan on June 1, 1950, No. 10800 worked south to Derby via Leeds, arriving there on June 30. Its first revenue career commenced on November 20, with a diagram that took in passenger trains on a Derby-Nottingham-Kettering triangle, before finishing its day with a trip from Derby to Manchester Central, returning with late night parcels train.

By December of that year it was allocated to Willesden shed in north London for trials in revenue earning service. It moved to Bletchley in 1951. A wide range of secondary passenger and lighter goods trains provided the mixed traffic locomotive with a variety of challenges.

Between July and December 1954, the locomotive was allocated to Brighton on the Southern Region for trials on various Central and South Eastern Section lines, measuring its capabilities against steam locomotives such as the SR's allocation of Fairburn 4MT 2-6-4Ts. However, its stay in the south was largely an unhappy one, with many failures reported, including a major engine failure

at Streatham Common on March 30, 1953 which put it out of action until December of that year. In December 1954 it moved to the Eastern Region at Plaistow in East London for trials on cross-London freight turns – a prelude to the early introduction of BR diesels on these duties from the late-1950s.

By February 1955, No. 10800 was back on the LMR where, perhaps surprisingly for a relatively low-powered machine, it spent time working a Rugby-based 5MT 4-6-0 cross-country diagram between Rugby, Peterborough and Birmingham, hauling trains of up to ten bogies on particularly busy days. It was also employed as station pilot at Rugby for a time.

Originally painted in gloss BR black with the lion and wheel emblem, by January 1957 it carried BR green with red bufferbeams and shanks.

Withdrawal came in August 1959, after which the locomotive was stored at Derby Works pending disposal. However, No. 10800 hadn't worked since February 1958. Performance was said to be 'lacklustre', although given some of the duties it was asked to perform, this may not have always been entirely the locomotive's fault.

But, No. 10800's experimental career was extended by Brush, which bought it in 1962 and rebuilt it as a testbed for new three-phase AC traction equipment. 'Project Hawk' was a collaboration between Brush and BR to develop AC alternators and traction motors in place of traditional DC equipment.

The Paxman power unit was replaced with a Bristol-Siddeley-Maybach MD655 unit, a spare from D0280 *Falcon* then on test with BR. The short bonnet end was completely rebuilt with sophisticated electronics replacing the train heating boiler.

Brush painted the locomotive in an all-over Sherwood green livery with brown bogies and the BR late emblem prior to its release from Loughborough, although unlike fellow Brush diesel prototypes *Falcon* and *Kestrel*, the locomotive never carried its name.

On-site testing took place at Loughborough throughout 1963-64 before No. 10800 – by now referred to as 'Hawk' by Brush – was inspected by BR and sent to Rugby Testing Station for static performance trials in 1965. Running trials took place on the former Great Central main line between Leicester and Nottingham between 1965 and 1968 when the project was abandoned. After several years dumped at Loughborough, the remains of No. 10800 were finally scrapped in 1972, except for the bogies which survived until May 1976, and

ABOVE: No. 10800 was withdrawn in August 1959, although it hadn't worked since February 1958. In April 1960 it was stored at Derby Works pending disposal but unlike the partially dismantled 'Fell' diesel behind, it would find further work. COLOUR-RAIL

the radiator section which could still be seen on site in September 1983.

However, experience gained with AC brushless alternators during the programme led to further developments, firstly with Class 47s D1960/61 in 1966, and then with later BR diesel classes, including the Class 43 HST power cars and Class 56, 58 and 60 freight locomotives. Many BR locomotives were also converted to

provide Electric Train Supply (ETS) using Brush AC main generators.

Two 'Pilot Scheme' designs that owed much to No. 10800 (in original form) were ordered by BR. Closest in appearance to the prototype were the deeply unsuccessful NBL/Paxman Type 1s D8400-09 (Class 16). More numerous, but scarcely more useful were Clayton/Paxman/BTH D8200-43, later designated as Class 15. ●

ABOVE: A rare view of No. 10800 at Loughborough in July 1966, after it was rebuilt as a testbed for new three-phase AC traction equipment. COLOUR-RAIL

More Power, More Speed

By the late-1950s, British Railways was looking for more powerful diesels to accelerate express services and move heavier freights. The prospect of large orders prompted several of the major locomotive builders to produce speculative prototypes for main line testing.

ABOVE: When *Deltic* was completed in 1955, diesel-electric locomotives were generally overweight and underpowered, unable to compete with the best and most powerful steam locomotives they were designed to replace. Between 1959 and 1961 it worked on the Eastern Region, paving the way for the 22 production Deltics on trains such as the London King's Cross-Leeds 'White Rose', seen here about to depart from the capital. COLOUR-RAIL

DELTIC:
EE's Game Changer

English Electric Diesel Prototype 1 – better known as DELTIC – wrapped two Napier gunboat engines in a striking bodyshell to produce what was, in 1955, the world's most powerful single unit diesel locomotive.

ABOVE: In June 1957, *Deltic* passes Halton Junction, near Runcorn, with the Euston-Liverpool Lime Street 'Merseyside Express'. Duties at this time included hauling named expresses such as 'The Shamrock', clocking up daily mileages of over 700 and working six days a week alongside Stanier 'Pacifics' on heavy WCML expresses. RAIL PHOTOPRINTS

The most remarkable diesel locomotive of its time, English Electric's *Deltic* was a purely speculative venture that went on to leave a lasting legacy on British motive power policy.

Unusually for a prototype that spent some years working on BR metals, *Deltic* was neither conceived nor requested by the national operator and it never carried a number. Unlike many locomotives and trains featured in this publication, it did lead to a high-profile production order and although EE would have hoped for more than the 22 locomotives it eventually built for BR, their impact on the 1960s railway scene was transformative.

When *Deltic* was completed in 1955, diesel-electric locomotives were generally overweight and underpowered, unable to compete with the best and most powerful steam locomotives they were designed to replace.

EE was keen to demonstrate that the compact, lightweight Napier-Deltic opposed piston diesel engine, already proven in marine applications such as Royal Navy fast gunboats, could be adapted for railway use. Their size and weight meant that two such engines, producing 1,600hp each, could be accommodated in a six-axle diesel locomotive weighing just over 100 tons. By contrast, Derby's 2,500hp 'Peaks' tipped the scales at 138t and required two extra unpowered axles to spread the weight, despite delivering 800hp less than EE's prototype!

Assembled at the Dick, Kerr Works in Preston, the 3,300hp locomotive was to have been named *Enterprise*, but emerged from works in October 1955 with the name *Deltic* applied to the blue body. With an eye on export orders, particularly in North America, EE clad the locomotive in a very striking bodyshell with large nose-mounted headlamps (never used) and a stunning bright blue livery with cream and gold lining.

On completion it was the most powerful single unit diesel locomotive in the world, offering the potential to greatly accelerate express passenger schedules without being penalised by the civil engineering

ABOVE: With a heavy train of ex-LMS and GWR stock in tow, *Deltic* crosses the Birdswood Flyover at Weaver Junction heading south on April 12, 1958. RAIL PHOTOPRINTS

department on weight grounds.

EE loaned the machine to BR London Midland Region initially, based at Liverpool's Edge Hill shed for static and running tests. This kept it close to its Vulcan Foundry birthplace in case of any problems. Its first main line outings were on overnight goods trains between Liverpool and London, with occasional passenger turns.

Deltic hauled its first passenger train on December 13, 1955, powering 'The Merseyside Express' from Liverpool Lime Street to London Euston.

The locomotive also visited the Settle-Carlisle line, which had a history of being used to put new locomotives through their paces. BR pushed the EE prototype in a series of tests on this route in September 1956, *Deltic* coping admirably with the challenges it was set. After minor modifications, October 1956 saw *Deltic* back in service between the capital and Liverpool. Duties included hauling named expresses such as 'The Shamrock' throughout 1957/58, and venturing north to Carlisle on occasions,

clocking up daily mileages of over 700 and working six days a week alongside Stanier 'Pacifics' on heavy WCML expresses.

However, as the LMR saw 25kV AC electrification as the future of the West Coast Main Line and had little use for such a powerful diesel locomotive, its future clearly lay elsewhere.

In 1959, the locomotive moved to the Eastern Region, based at Hornsey in north London for further trials. Although its width and bodyshell profile caused some gauging issues in the north-east, where it came into contact with certain platform edges, test runs on the GN Section and in Scotland were a success and the ER quickly saw *Deltic*'s potential. Thanks to the efforts of ER General Manager Gerard Fiennes, an order for production 'Deltics' was placed in 1958 – with 22 locomotives expected to replace no fewer than 55 ex-LNER 'Pacifics' on East Coast Main Line expresses.

The gauging problems restricted *Deltic* to former Great Northern Railway main routes between Kings Cross, Doncaster and Leeds, and even to certain platforms

at 'the Cross', but between 1959 and 1961 it acquitted itself well on the ECML.

Various modifications were made, based on experience in service, including raising the maximum speed from 90mph to 106mph, a pace *Deltic* proved more than capable of achieving and maintaining over the ECML racetrack! Giving a foretaste of what was to come with the production 'Deltics', the prototype underwent several power unit changes and a serious engine failure while running at high speed led to its withdrawal from front line service in March 1961.

With the production locomotives starting to arrive, it was returned to EE's Vulcan Foundry at Newton-le-Willows, pending a decision on its future. After an external restoration to pristine condition, it was presented to the Science Museum in London, where it arrived by road on April 28, 1963.

For 30 years it was resident in South Kensington, alongside other groundbreaking machines, before being moved to the National Railway Museum in York in 1993. In the years since, it has also been displayed at Locomotion in Shildon and at Barrow Hill's Deltic Depot alongside its six surviving production batch descendents. Sadly, there appears to be no prospect of it ever running under its own power again.

Despite being capable of startling speed and haulage power for its time, *Deltic* could easily have remained a one-off without the persistence of Gerard Fiennes. Although the hoped-for export orders never materialised, the impact of the production 'Deltics', bringing regular 100mph operation to Britain for the first time, should not be underestimated. The gains made by the Class 55s set the benchmark for BR's subsequent high-speed diesel trains and proved that diesels could deliver serious reductions in schedules on lines where electrification was not imminent. ●

ABOVE: On the Eastern Region, *Deltic's* performance convinced management that it needed a fleet of production machines to replace the ex-LNER 'Pacifics' on East Coast Main Line expresses. In 1959, the prototype passes Werrington, north of Peterborough with an Up express for King's Cross. M.W. EARLEY/RAILWAY MAGAZINE ARCHIVE

FAMOUS FOUR: THE 1960s DIESEL PROTOTYPES

With large orders for more powerful Type 4 and Type 5 diesels on the horizon, Britain's leading locomotive builders invested heavily in speculative prototypes in the 1960s.

English Electric DP2

It may have looked like a Deltic, but it had the 16-cylinder heart of what would later become Class 50. English Electric's Diesel Prototype 2 (DP2) was regarded as the most successful of the three 'second generation' Type 4 demonstrators tested by BR from 1961/62. Even after the decision to build hundreds of Brush Type 4s (Class 47s), the locomotive was retained by British Railways and worked alongside the Eastern Region's Deltic fleet until it was written off in a collision in July 1967. By that stage, BR had already asked English Electric to supply 50 locomotives

developed from the DP2 concept to help accelerate West Coast Main Line Anglo-Scottish expresses prior to electrification.

Dissatisfied with its first generation of Type 4 (2,000hp+) diesel locomotives, BR made it known in the early-1960s that it was looking for more powerful mixed traffic machines of around 2,700hp. These would allow it to accelerate and/or increase the weight of passenger and freight trains to make them more efficient.

Faced with the prospect of a lucrative order for several hundred locomotives, Britain's locomotive builders were keen to show that they could deliver a

machine that met BR's specification.

Three privately-built prototype main line locomotives were built by English Electric, Brush and BRCW/AEI, but Brush was also building a batch of 20 Type 4 Co-Cos developed from the Derby/Sulzer 1-Co-Co-1s (later Class 46).

English Electric's contribution was DP2, with a new 2,700hp, 16-cylinder turbocharged engine housed in a modified Deltic body. Two large radiator grilles at the No. 1 end on each side were most obvious external evidence that this wasn't a Deltic. Outshopped in plain, dark BR green with small yellow

ABOVE: In August 1963 DP2 waits for departure time at King's Cross with a northbound East Coast Main Line express. Despite being less powerful than the production Class 55s it resembled, it came to be regarded as the '23rd Deltic' and was well thought of by ER crews. RAIL PHOTOPRINTS

ABOVE: Working regular EE Type 4 (Class 40) diagrams from Euston to Liverpool and Crewe, and later Euston-Carlisle, DP2 quickly proved its superiority over the ponderous 1-Co-Co-1 design, and gained an enviable reputation for reliability, clocking up 164,600 miles in 13 months. In July 1962 it passes Weaver Junction with a southbound express. RAIL PHOTOPRINTS

warning panels, the locomotive initially ran trials on the London Midland Region, based at Camden in north London.

Using a number of 'off-the-shelf' components from its Type 3 and Type 5 production runs, including traction motors and bogies, EE was able to build its demonstrator relatively cheaply, and the similarity to existing classes meant that DP2 was more readily accepted by BR's operating department than the more advanced *Falcon* and *Lion*.

May 2, 1962 saw the locomotive make its first proving runs from Vulcan Foundry to Chester and back, and after tests and crew training it entered revenue earning service with the London Midland Region at Camden just 12 days later. Working regular EE Type 4 (Class 40) diagrams from Euston to Liverpool and Crewe, and later Euston-Carlisle, the locomotive quickly proved its superiority over the ponderous 1-Co-Co-1 design, and gained an enviable reputation for reliability, clocking up 164,600 miles in 13 months.

DP2 returned to Vulcan Foundry for overhaul in May 1963. When it re-emerged it was sent to the Eastern Region where it worked alongside the ER's Deltic fleet on a diagram encompassing turns to Newcastle and Edinburgh.

From winter 1963, the locomotive moved its own diagram on the Leeds route, including the 'Yorkshire Pullman'. By early-1964 it was being used on the King's Cross-Sheffield 'Master Cutler' diagram.

As with the Deltic fleet, DP2's bogies were changed from fabricated to cast steel in late-1963 as these were better suited to the punishment inflicted by regular high-speed running. At its next works visit in April 1965, DP2 was repainted in Deltic style two-tone green and was subsequently hired to BR, based at Tinsley depot in Sheffield. From there it continued to work the 'Cutler' and the 11.20pm Tinsley-King's Cross goods until being taken out of service in January 1966.

By this time, BR had ordered 50 Type 4s based on DP2, albeit with an advanced electronic control system and other features which were tested on the prototype. Once these were in place, DP2 returned to traffic with the ER hauling trains including the Holloway-Edinburgh car carrier and King's Cross-Cambridge expresses.

David N. Clough reports in his book *Diesel Pioneers* that only nine 'on the road' failures were reported between 1962 and 1967, during which time the locomotive covered just over 607,000 miles. A failure rate of 19,000 miles per casualty was "appreciably higher than either a Deltic or a Class 50."

Such was DP2's reliability that the Eastern Region felt confident enough to diagram it alongside the Class 55 Deltic fleet, and this continued until July 31, 1967 when the locomotive met its untimely end. While standing in for a Deltic on the 12.00 King's Cross-Edinburgh express, DP2 collided with a derailed cement train at speed near Thirsk and was severely damaged. Although the driver and secondman escaped injury, the collision killed seven people and injured 45 others.

The wrecked locomotive was removed to Vulcan Foundry, where it was eventually scrapped in 1970 after being stripped for spares. Its power unit went into the Class 50 pool and saw many more years of service until the class was withdrawn in the early-1990s.

ABOVE: DP2, *Lion* and *Falcon* were entrusted with the 'Master Cutler' and 'Sheffield Pullman' services during their ER trials. On September 24, 1965 DP2, by now in two-tone green, stands at Sheffield Victoria after arrival with the 1120 midday working from King's Cross. PETER HOGARTH/RAILWAY MAGAZINE ARCHIVE

WHITE HEAT: BRCW D0260 *LION*

ABOVE: Making an extraordinary contrast with the filthy black and green steam locomotives and dark green diesels of the time, a spotless white and gold D0260 *Lion* passes Shrewsbury during a proving run in April 1962. RAIL PHOTOPRINTS

Has there ever been a more striking diesel locomotive on the British railway? D0260 *Lion* might have lasted less than two years, but this demonstrator built by Birmingham Railway Carriage & Wagon Co. (BRCW) and AEI must have been a remarkable sight. Its bright white livery was a world away from the filthy steam locomotives of the time. Although impractical for regular squadron service, *Lion*'s external appearance was in keeping with the spirit of the early-1960s, with its emphasis on modernity, progress and technological change. However, the bankruptcy of BRCW in 1964 condemned the locomotive to a swift end.

While English Electric provided DP2, and Brush's contribution was *Falcon*, The Birmingham Railway Carriage &

Wagon Co., along with Associated Electrical Industries (AEI) and Sulzer Brothers of Switzerland, produced what would prove to be BRCW's final locomotive design – the 2,750hp Sulzer-powered *Lion*. Mechanically, *Lion* was similar to the Brush Type 4 Co-Co that would become Class 47 – it had a derivative of the same Sulzer 12LDA28 engine and even looked relatively similar.

D0260 was ahead of its time – being fitted with electric train supply (as well as a Spanner Mk 3 steam-heat boiler). ETS was a feature already proven in service on the BRCW Type 3s for the Southern Region.

The front end featured a four-character headcode, two Class 27/33-style red tail lights and a handrail that was vertical at the sides and curved to run horizontally below the two front cab windows. The

cab design was based on the Type 2 – certainly on the sides. It was vacuum-braked only, perhaps a strange decision given that the Class 33s were dual-braked from new from 1960.

Lion was delivered in April 1962 and tested until September of that year when it returned to BRCW.

Numbered D0260, the locomotive ran trials on the Western Region, initially based at Wolverhampton Stafford Road and used on Paddington-Birmingham Snow Hill route. It was later tested between Paddington and Swindon, on the fearsome south Devon banks and on the 1-in-37 Lickey Incline, where it famously restarted a 20-coach test train.

It was back on test with BR in April 1963 and spent several months in traffic on the Eastern Region, working prestige trains such as the 'Yorkshire Pullman' and 'Master Cutler' until a serious failure in January 1964. With BRCW in terminal financial difficulty, *Lion* was sent to Doncaster Works for examination and then to AEI in Attercliffe, Sheffield (BRCW's electrical contractor) in 1964 for dismantling. After the electrical equipment and Sulzer engine had been recovered, the body was scrapped by T.W. Ward at nearby Beighton later that year, or possibly in 1965. Strangely for such a distinctive, high-profile machine, little is known about its demise.

Although it ran only 80,000 miles in 18 months of sporadic activity, *Lion* provided BR with valuable experience and information that was incorporated into the 512 Brush Type 4s, especially with regard to engines and traction equipment.

• For more on D0260 *Lion*, see www.class47.co.uk

ABOVE: During its time on the Eastern Region, *Lion* stands in Doncaster Works yard in October 1963. A few months later it was withdrawn and quietly dismantled. COLOUR-RAIL

ABOVE: After spending 1964 in store, BR hired D0280 from Brush and it moved to the Western Region in January 1965, based at Bristol Bath Road. The locomotive was a regular on Paddington-Bristol and South Wales expresses, working alongside the 'Westerns' and Brush Type 4s to which it was closely related. In April 1967 D0280 gets ready for departure from Bristol Temple Meads. RAIL PHOTOPRINTS

BRUSH'S TWIN-ENGINE CONTENDER: D0280 *FALCON*

D0280 *Falcon* employed modified Class 31 bogies and cab details and twin Maybach MD655 engines as used in the 'Western' class diesel-hydraulics. However, in this case, the high-speed diesel engines were allied to a diesel-electric transmission rather than hydraulic drive.

Falcon was completed in September 1961 and made its main line debut on the Eastern Region the following month. Initial trials on the East Coast and Great Eastern Main Lines were followed by a spell on test on the Western Region, where the prototype was compared with the region's 'Westerns'. A unique livery, described as 'lime green and chestnut brown' was applied, complete with orange bufferbeams.

During summer 1962 and 1963 the locomotive was based at Sheffield's Darnall depot and used on the 'Master Cutler' and 'Sheffield Pullman' services, briefly moving to work coal traffic between the Nottinghamshire coalfield and East Anglia in late-1962. After spending 1964 in store, BR agreed to hire D0280 from Brush and the

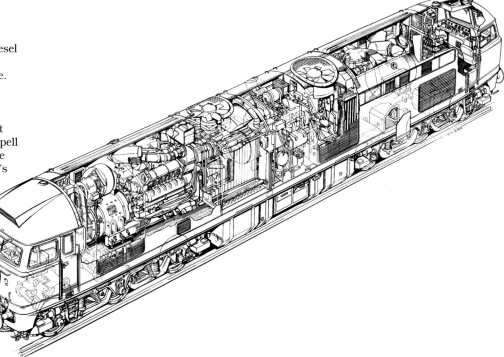

ABOVE: Cutaway technical diagram of D0280 *Falcon*. RAILWAY MAGAZINE ARCHIVE

locomotive transferred to the Western Region in January 1965, being based at Bristol Bath Road. Prior to its move south, Brush repainted the locomotive in darker BR green with a light green solebar stripe.

The locomotive was a regular on Paddington-Bristol and South Wales expresses, working alongside the 'Westerns' and Brush Type 4s to which it was closely related.

In April 1970, *Falcon* was overhauled again and swapped its vacuum brake equipment for air brake capability. This allowed it to be used on BR's then-new Mk 2a/b/c stock, which was being introduced on Western Region front-line trains at the time. It was also repainted BR blue during this works visit. Surprisingly, BR bought the locomotive from Brush in December 1970 and renumbered it 1200.

However, its stint on Inter-City passenger work ended when the locomotive was transferred to Ebbw Junction depot in Newport in July 1972. From then until withdrawal in October 1975, *Falcon* eked out a living hauling unfitted freights in South Wales. It was scrapped by Cashmore's of Newport in March 1976.

• For a detailed history of D0280, see www.class47.co.uk/c47_feature_424.php

ABOVE: *Falcon* finished its career working freight trains in South Wales. Between 1972 and 1975 it was based at Ebbw Junction in Newport, where it was captured shortly before withdrawal alongside a fellow Brush product. COLOUR-RAIL

BIG BIRD: HS4000 *KESTREL*

The strange life of HS4000 *Kestrel* is a fascinating story that comes with a whiff of intrigue. Built by Brush in 1968, HS4000 was – and remains – the most powerful single-engine diesel locomotive ever to run on BR; its Sulzer 16-cylinder 16LVA24 engine developed almost 4,000hp. The locomotive was also one of the first in Britain to employ the latest AC traction motor technology.

It's no surprise that HS4000 had a similar body to a Class 47, but its cabs were radically altered with a curved front end to give a more streamlined look. This was presumably because HS4000 was designed for 125mph running.

Livery was a golden yellow upper body and a chocolate-brown lower half split by a white waist stripe, with mid-grey roof, red bufferbeams and black underframe, bogies and bufferbeam fairings. Four-character headcode boxes were provided underneath the raked-back cab windows and marker lights were an unattractive protruding design. Cumbersome roof-mounted horns were also fitted. Buffers were mounted on two protruding columns to give the locomotive a distinctive, powerful appearance.

Hawker Siddeley (by now the parent company of Brush) logos and branding were applied under the driver's cabside windows and *Kestrel* branding on the central portion of the bodyside. On

one side, a two-piece ventilation grille was added low on the bodyside, and apart from the full-height engine room access door, the bodyside was smooth and uninterrupted like a Class 47 – albeit without the small windows.

BR rarely tested the locomotive to anywhere near its full capability, but May 8, 1968 gave an illustration of what it could do. Hauling a train of 20 Mk 1 coaches weighing around 665 tons, *Kestrel* topped Shap Summit on the West Coast Main Line at 46mph. That August the locomotive hauled what was then BR's heaviest ever train, 2,028t, formed of HAA 'merry-go-round' coal hoppers. Either side of these special tests the locomotive

ABOVE: One of *Kestrel's* final public appearances was at Barrow Hill depot open day in 1971. At this time the 4,000hp prototype was based at nearby Shirebrook hauling coal trains on a regular diagram to Whitemoor Yard. COLOUR-RAIL

employed on a regular freight diagram hauling 1,600t vacuum-braked coal trains from Shirebrook in the Nottinghamshire coalfield to Whitemoor Yard near March.

Kestrel was dual-braked and had electric train supply (ETS) from new – the jumper cable being mounted on the cab front. In February 1969, HS4000 lost its original, heavyweight Commonwealth bogies for Class 47-style bogies, reducing its axle load in the process. This was to enable it to work 100mph passenger trains, which it did on the East Coast Main Line for a short period, from October 1969 to March 1970. A regular diagram saw the locomotive stand in for a Class 55 on the 0755 King's Cross-Newcastle and 1645 return. Availability was said to be excellent and speeds of over 100mph were recorded. After its high speed exploits, *Kestrel* returned to its regular Shirebrook-Whitemoor diagrams until early 1971. *Kestrel* was withdrawn in March 1971 and – somewhat surprisingly considering the political situation of the time – sold to the Soviet Union.

Pictures of it in Russia are exceptionally rare – although one view shows it working with a massive roof-mounted headlight on just one end! Even when in Russia, it retained its headcode roller blinds – this view showing 3S74 being displayed. *Kestrel* was tested against Soviet TEP60 passenger locomotives, presumably with a view to incorporating Brush technology into the next generation of diesels.

It's hard to say if HS4000 was re-liveried; the quality of the pictures seems to suggest it was not repainted and even retained its HS4000 number and *Kestrel* names. It appears its vacuum brakes were removed, but ETS (jumpers at least) was retained. A standard Russian knuckle type auto-coupler was fitted to enable it

to haul trains on the 5ft gauge network.

Information about *Kestrel's* life in Russia is scarce as it was during the 'Cold War' when details were hard to come by, but it is thought to have spent its time as a test locomotive right through to 1988. It is understood to have been broken up as recently as the summer of 1993.

ABOVE: On April 19, 1970 an unusually dirty HS4000 sits in the depot yard at Hull Dairycoates. After a period on 100mph East Coast Main Line expresses, working in a Deltic diagram, the locomotive returned to freight duty in 1970/71. RAIL PHOTOPRINTS

Experimental BR Diesels

Locomotives are occasionally modified to test new equipment, engines or assess them for a change of use, as this selection of BR and ex-BR diesels shows.

ABOVE: No. 47046 was a testbed for many years, first receiving a Class 56 engine and becoming No. 47601 in late-1975 and then a 'guinea pig' for the Class 58 project in 1980. As No. 47901 it was a 3,300hp Type 5 and worked alongside Class 56s on heavy freight trains in the south of England until withdrawal in 1990. On July 7, 1988 it was in charge of an ARC stone train passing Warminster. RAIL PHOTOPRINTS

LEFT: In preparation for the stillborn Class 38 project, six Class 37/0s were rebuilt with new Mirrlees MB275T (Nos. 37901-904) and Ruston RK270T (Nos. 37905/906) power units in parallel with the major '37' refurbishment programme of the mid-1980s. They were allocated to heavy steel traffic in South Wales, as seen in this view of No. 37902 and a sister machine passing Cardiff Central with a Llanwern-Port Talbot iron ore train on May 22, 1990. RAIL PHOTOPRINTS

ABOVE: No. 50049 *Defiance* was modified for 80mph operation in 1987 and tested on stone trains around Westbury. The trial was not a success and, after a period on Cornish china clay work, No. 50149 returned to 100mph passenger work with Network SouthEast in 1989. During its Westbury trials, the unique Railfreight machine slogs up the bank at Upton Scudamore, near Warminster, on October 18, 1987. JOHN CHALCRAFT

ABOVE: After privatisation in the mid-1990s, the new rolling stock leasing companies and freight operators looked at various options for modernising the ex-BR diesel fleet. In 1998/99, Brush refurbished and re-engineered 12 Freightliner Class 47s with General Motors engines as Class 57. As a trial for passenger work, Brush also converted Porterbrook's No. 47825 into Electric Train Supply (ETS) fitted No. 57601. While on hire to First Great Western, the striking purple and silver demonstrator passes North Brewham in Somerset on June 27, 2002. JOHN CHALCRAFT

LEFT: During the 1960s, various BR diesels were modified to test new equipment or as testbeds for more powerful engines. English Electric Type 4 No. D255 was the only one of its class to receive Electric Train Heating (ETH) equipment for a short period in the early-1960s, as a prelude to its wider adoption on passenger stock. RAIL PHOTOPRINTS ●

Birth Of An Icon: BR's High Speed Diesel Train

BR's InterCity 125 brought new levels of comfort and speed to Britain's railways, marrying proven technology with infrastructure improvements and clever marketing.

ABOVE: On July 26, 1975, HST prototype No. 252001 heads away from Twerton Tunnel, between Bath and Bristol, during its period of revenue earning service on the Paddington-Bristol route. These early runs helped the Western Region to gather vital operational experience with 125mph trains prior to the October 1976 launch of the production trains. RAIL PHOTOPRINTS

The High Speed Train – or InterCity 125 HST – is a true railway icon. Its distinctive appearance – with an almost aggressive 'no nonsense' sloping nose – has made it a familiar sight to just about everybody who lives in the UK. There are likely to be few who have not travelled on one.

After more than 40 years, the HST is still in the front line and looks set to be so until at least the late-2020s. Simply, it is too good a train to go to the scrapyard.

When it was introduced, it was an immediate success on the Western Region and helped BR win back many of the passengers lost to road and air in previous years. East Coast Main Line (ECML), West of England, Midland Main Line and Cross-Country passengers also benefited from

the HST revolution as a total of 95 trains were introduced between 1976 and 1983.

InterCity under threat

By the late-1960s British Rail's Inter-City brand was well established but starting to suffer from serious competition from the growing network of motorways and air travel. Locomotive-hauled trains, often formed of vacuum-braked, steam-heated Mk 1 stock, were the backbone of BR's long-distance business. Although the introduction of Mk 2 stock in 1965 and the subsequent development of the air-conditioned Mk 2d-f fleets improved matters, there was a pressing need for higher speeds to make rail travel more attractive and competitive.

Building completely new high-speed lines, such as Japanese *Shinkansen*, was not considered viable in the UK, but BR's research department was working on proposals for a train that could tilt to increase speeds through corners on existing lines. Although the experimental Advanced Passenger Train (APT) was authorised in 1969, it was quickly realised that the concept would take years to develop fully.

At the rate long-distance passengers were switching to their cars or the airlines, BR could not wait years for a new high-speed train, however innovative or effective it could eventually be.

By 1970 BRB Chairman Sir Henry Johnson and Chief Mechanical and Electrical Engineer (CM&EE) Terry Miller were well

ABOVE: In March 1976, No. 252001 speeds through Sonning Cutting, near Reading, with a test run. RAIL PHOTOPRINTS

to keep its weight around the same as a Mk 2. However, much of the coach was developed from the Mk 2, using its best parts and learning from its weaknesses.

HST power cars would also use existing technology. A Paxman Valenta diesel engine, developed from the Ventura engine used in the North British Class 29 locomotive, was chosen for its high power-to-weight ratio. There were worries about using this engine as it had not been a great success in the '29s' and the locomotives were withdrawn after a few years' service. Although there have been some problems with the engines over the years, it has stood up remarkably well to the intense high-speed, stop-start work performed by the HST.

A Brush traction package, developed from that used in the 4,000hp Brush prototype *Kestrel*, was chosen and has also proved to be successful. Two-axle bogies, developed from those fitted experimentally to 25kV electric locomotive E3173 for high-speed tests in the late 1960s, would carry the power cars. Incidentally, during the tests E3173 carried a glass-fibre streamlined nose of a similar design to the one that would be fitted to the prototype HST.

On June 11, 1972 the first prototype HST power car, 41001, was completed at Crewe and sent to the RTC at Derby, followed in August by 41002. Eight Mk 3 trailer vehicles were completed at Litchurch Lane works in Derby between March and July, with two catering vehicles completed later. The full set then underwent static testing at Derby before moving to the RTC's test track at Old Dalby.

Union problems

However, in the summer of 1972, train drivers' union ASLEF objected to the cab design of the new train with its single central driving position and demanded that any train operating above 100mph had to be double-manned with the drivers sitting side-by-side.

Almost before it had turned a wheel, the HSDT found itself 'blacked' after ASLEF discovered that the prototype was being tested at Old Dalby. Running tests were suspended until December 1972 when a compromise was reached. Although the dispute prevented any main line testing, the opportunity was taken to carry out static tests at the RTC.

In January 1973 the HST made its first main line appearance, No. 41002 working Derby-Wigston Junction-Lenton Junction-Derby test trains. Using one power car meant that the train had to be turned on the triangular junctions at Wigston and Lenton before returning to Derby. Meanwhile, 41001 was undergoing static ride tests at the RTC.

The first outing of the complete prototype HST was in February 1973 when it made a trip from Derby to Wellingborough. A warning of what was to become a common HST problem was given early in the trip when a turbocharger on one of the power cars blew at Spondon and the journey had to be completed on one power car. However, this did highlight the 'belt-and-braces' benefits of having two power cars.

At the end of February the train moved

aware that APT was a long-term solution and turned to a less radical project known as the High Speed Diesel Train (HSDT).

A pro-active working group was established involving designers, vehicle constructors, train operators, marketing experts and even representatives of the parcels department! All members of the HSDT team worked together to provide a common solution to all their needs in what proved to be the last full prototyping arrangement for a UK train. A good example of this co-operation are the bodyside air intakes on the power cars which were modified on the production trains to improve air intake while giving a more streamlined appearance.

HSDT, later shortened to HST, was to use proven technology wherever possible but upgraded to achieve 125mph running

on existing infrastructure. Authorisation to develop a prototype HST was given by BRB in August 1970 and just 22 months later in June 1972, the train was ready to begin trials at the Railway Technical Centre (RTC) in Derby.

Proven technology

BR engineers at the RTC had already been working on a replacement for the Mk 2 coach before the HST project started and this vehicle – the Mk 3 – would form the passenger accommodation for the new train, with seven or eight trailers sandwiched between two 2,250hp diesel locomotives or power cars. The Mk 3 was the longest vehicle ever built for UK service at 22.15 metres (75ft) and used lightweight materials

ABOVE: After the introduction of the production Inter-City 125s in 1976, the prototype set was disbanded and the power cars were used by BR's Railway Technical Centre in Derby. On July 26, 1977 one of the two prototype power cars passes Chesterfield with two RTC test vehicles and an APT-P electric power car. JOHN CHALCRAFT

to Neville Hill depot in Leeds for more main line tests. At this time the project was being hindered by a lack of suitable facilities and Neville Hill was the only depot in the country with a building long enough to accommodate the train. Also, a complete absence of 125mph railway meant that the train could not yet show its full capabilities.

Once again ASLEF 'blacked' the train in February, preventing its use, although by April the issue had been resolved by fitting a secondman's seat behind the central driver's position.

On May 3, 1973 HST made its debut on the ECML with a test run to Hitchin. The persistent union problems meant that in the year since their delivery No. 41001 had run just 3,273 miles and No. 41002 had reached 7,000 miles.

July 1973 saw the train finally start to show its paces on a series of test runs on the ECML 'race track' between York and Darlington. On July 7, 131mph was achieved, followed by 140, 141 and a world record-breaking 143mph on July 12.

A significant day for the HST project was August 2, 1973 when the train ran empty from Leeds to King's Cross for a press trip to Darlington and return. According to one member of the HST team, the train ran faultlessly, even proving the strength of its windscreens when a piece of ballast flew up at over 125mph. The success of the press trip attracted the interest of the Government, which was vital if funding for a production series of HSTs was to be granted.

From August 20 the train covered 709 miles a day on a regular Leeds-Edinburgh-Newcastle-Edinburgh-Leeds diagram. It was planned to carry passengers on the 'North

Briton' Leeds-Edinburgh and return sections, but once again problems with the unions meant that drivers would not drive the train with passengers on board, so it ran empty to accumulate 100,000 miles necessary before the design could be finalised.

The HST revolution

In the spring of 1974 the HST moved to the Western Region for tests in preparation for the introduction of the production fleet between Paddington, Bristol and South Wales.

As part of the HST project, BR civil engineers were upgrading Brunel's main line to the West to make it suitable for 125mph running. Fortunately, the superb engineering of the route made it ideal. Another reason for choosing this route was the M4, which was 'bleeding the Western Region to death', according to one BR source.

During tests the HST concept proved itself more than capable of fulfilling the role it was created for. The 4,500hp installed gave the train enough power to maintain schedule, even with eight vehicles rather than the planned seven. It was also found that it could brake from 125mph in a shorter distance than a normal locomotive-hauled train could from 100mph, removing the need for an expensive resignalling programme.

On May 5, 1975 the prototype HST – by now numbered 252001– went into revenue-earning service between London and Bristol, its first working being the 07.45 Bristol Parkway-Paddington, paving the way for the full HST service just over a year later.

Preparations for the new trains were being made during this period with dedicated new depots at St Philip's Marsh in Bristol

and Old Oak Common in west London. New facilities were also provided at Cardiff Canton and Landore depot in Swansea. As the HST revolution spread to other parts of the network, new depots were also built at Bounds Green in London, Craigentinny (Edinburgh), Heaton (Newcastle), Neville Hill (Leeds) and Laira in Plymouth.

Apart from some tidying-up work and improvements needed following experience with the prototype, the production sets were very similar to No. 252001, illustrating how good the initial concept was. Technical changes included a hydraulic parking brake rather than the traditional handbrake and the adoption of a three-phase train supply system instead of the standard 850V system used on other BR stock. This eliminated the need for motor alternator sets in each coach, saving weight and, in the longer term, money.

In 2017, HST is still in service with Great Western Railway (GWR), Virgin Trains East Coast, CrossCountry, East Midlands Trains and Network Rail, although many sets will be displaced by new Hitachi Intercity Express Train (IET) bi-mode units over the next couple of years. However, 27 sets are moving to ScotRail to improve internal Scottish services between Glasgow, Edinburgh, Inverness and Aberdeen, while some will continue with GWR and other operators for years to come.

Of the original train, power car No. 41001 is preserved in full working order, No. 41002 was scrapped in the late-1980s. Almost all of the trailers are still in regular use with passenger operators or as Network Rail test car or Royal Train vehicles. Without question, the prototype HST must be regarded as one of the most successful experimental trains of all time. ●

Railcar Renaissance

Originally designed to be the saviour of rural branch lines, diesel railcars and railbuses have become the dominant form of traction away from electrified routes since the 1980s, thanks to a series of experimental prototypes.

Even before the Second World War, many branch lines around Britain were failing to cover their costs. For rural districts where passenger traffic was sparse, railway companies developed many different solutions to reduce operating costs; from steam railmotors and push-pull trains to railcars powered by internal combustion engines – at the time a relatively new form of traction for railways.

Necessity, as always, proved to be the mother of invention and some of the poorest railway companies – most notably those running narrow gauge lines in north-west Ireland – devised cheap, efficient diesel railbuses that eventually inspired the British railcar revolution (see page 52). But, as car ownership increased and passenger numbers continued to dwindle, more radical solutions were needed if lines were to stay open.

Under similar circumstances, simple, lightweight railbuses were developed for rural light railways in Germany from the 1920s onwards, for both standard and narrow gauge use. In the early-1950s West German state railway Deutsche Bundesbahn took on the idea and introduced a series of prototype 4w railbuses and trailers.

Much cheaper to operate than conventional trains, the concept was very successful and production eventually ran to more than 800 units of various designs. Economical to run and requiring fewer staff to operate, they transformed service on secondary and branch lines all over the country. Their low-slung design and retractable steps also meant that they could stop almost anywhere, like a road bus, attracting new business from passengers who could board and alight at small halts and road crossings and buy tickets from the driver.

Despite visits to see the West German railbuses, BR took some years to acknowledge their potential for loss-making rural lines, preferring heavier diesel railcars instead.

ABOVE: Its Leyland National bus origins clearly visible, BR railbus prototype LEV1 was the progenitor of a series of lightweight railbuses introduced in the 1980s. RAILWAY MAGAZINE ARCHIVE

However, in mid-1956 authorisation was given for an experimental batch of around 20 diesel railbuses for trial use on Scottish, Eastern, Western and London Midland Region lines under threat of closure. Of those, five each were built by Park Royal, Wickham, AC Cars and German company Waggon und Maschinenbau of Donaueschingen and two by Bristol with Eastern Coachworks bodies.

While the railbuses proved cheaper to run and more popular with passengers than the elderly steam-hauled trains they replaced, reliability and durability were major issues. Failures were common, some railbuses even broke their frames and, weighing in at just 15t, collisions with obstructions on the line led to derailments. By March 1960, the British Transport Commission had decided that no more would be ordered. All had been withdrawn by 1968 and it appeared that the railbus revolution was over almost before it began.

Railbuses return

However, a decade after the original DRBs had disappeared from the network, a need for cheap new trains led BR to look at lightweight railbuses again.

In 1978, a strange looking hybrid of bus and rail technology emerged from BR's Railway Technical Centre (RTC) in Derby. Known as Leyland Experimental Vehicle 1, or LEV1 for short, it combined the modular body of the Leyland National bus with a two-axle underframe developed as part of the High Speed Freight Vehicle (HSFV) programme.

Initially tested as an unpowered vehicle, LEV1 later received a 200hp Leyland TL11 diesel engine, fully automatic SCG gearbox and a Gmeinder final drive unit on one axle.

LEV1 was the first of five prototype railbuses built by BR/Leyland in the late-1970s and early-1980s. It also ran in passenger service on various lines from 1983, before becoming part of the RTC test fleet. It is now part of the National Collection, although it is normally on loan to preserved railways.

LEV2 was exported to the USA and is now preserved in Connecticut while RB3 was built in 1981, tested on BR and resembled a Leyland National Mk 2 bus. In 1982 it was converted to 5ft 3in gauge and sold to Northern Ireland Railways.

RB002/004 of 1984 featured narrower bodies and stronger cab ends for railway use. RB002 was also tested in the USA and Canada, but also spent time in the Netherlands, Denmark and Sweden in an attempt to win export orders. RB004 resembles a single car version of the production Class 141s introduced in the same year. A two-car demonstrator, described as an 'economy version' of Class 141, was also built and exported to Thailand in 1984. It was also tested in Malaysia and Indonesia.

Work on the lightweight railbuses led to a more heavy-duty version being developed in 1979-81. Built to meet BR's more stringent crashworthiness rules, the unique two-car Class 140 toured the BR network from June 1981, from Cornwall to Scotland, building experience for the

ABOVE: LEV1 was followed by several more prototypes, including RB3, based on the Leyland National Mk 2 bodyshell. R3 was tested in the Bristol area in 1982 – seen here at Stapleton Road on April 22 of that year – before being sold to Northern Ireland Railways and regauged. COLOUR-RAIL

ABOVE: A rare view of export version RB002 on the main line in the UK, trundling down the East Coast Main Line at Copmanthorpe, near York. This railbus was also tested in Canada, the USA, Denmark and Sweden. COLOUR-RAIL

ABOVE: The more substantial two-car demonstrator No. 140001 at Middlesbrough on November 5, 1981. This unique railbus visited most corners of the BR network in the early-1980s and is now preserved in Scotland. RAIL PHOTOPRINTS

ABOVE: Heavy duty: diesel-electric prototype No. 210001 passes Midgham on the Reading-Newbury line with a crew training run from Westbury to Reading on April 29, 1982. MARION CANNING/RAILWAY MAGAZINE ARCHIVE

ABOVE: Single railbus RB004 closely resembles the production BRE/Leyland Class 141 two-car sets introduced in 1984. It is now preserved in working order at the Whitrope Heritage Centre in Scotland. RAILWAY MAGAZINE ARCHIVE

circles; first was a heavy-duty diesel-electric multiple unit based on the then-new Class 317 EMU. Intended for busy suburban and commuter diesel routes, such as the Thames Valley, two Class 210 prototypes were built at Derby Works in 1981. No.210001 was a four-car set powered by a Paxman 1,125hp engine while No. 210002 was a three-car unit with a 1,140hp MTU power unit. Their engines were mounted above the floor of a Driving Motor Second car, with the other vehicles being trailer cars, much like the Southern Region DEMUs of the 1950s and 1960s.

The '210s' were tested in various parts of the country, but eventually settled at Reading to work Paddington suburban routes to Reading, Oxford and Slough between 1983 and 1985. However, they were regarded by BR management as too heavy, too expensive and too complex for its requirements and by 1988 they had been withdrawn.

The '210' vehicles have led interesting lives since; two driving trailers, No. 210002's intermediate trailer and a trailer from No. 210001 were reformed to create the Class 457 'Networker' EMU development train (see page 121), the two driving cars of which are now preserved.

One of the TSOs is currently in South Western Railway Class 455 EMU set No. 455912 and the other two have been scrapped. DTSO No. 67301 from No. 210002 is currently in EMU No. 455913 following repairs.

Sprinting Ahead

The second concept for new BR DMUs took a much more conventional approach, choosing to build what was effectively a 1980s update of the original BR railcar concept.

BREL York built two prototypes in 1984, Nos. 150001/002, based on the Mk 3 bodyshell then being used for hundreds of Class 317-322 EMU vehicles. The two three-car sets had underfloor Cummins engines and Voith hydraulic transmission (150001) and Rolls-Royce engines with SCG mechanical gearboxes (150002), air-operated sliding doors and modern, open saloons.

They initially went to Derby RTC, where as part of the test programme, the units entered service on the Matlock branch. No. 150001 proved to be remarkably reliable and was used on various nationwide tests and promotional tours.

Given the unit's success, a production fleet of 50 Class 150/1s was quickly ordered, being deployed at Derby and later Tyseley, where they were joined by No. 150001 by 1987.

No. 150002's mechanical arrangement proved much less suitable and it spent some time out of service before being rebuilt as 90mph 'Sprinter Express' prototype No. 154002 in 1987. In this guise it gained Voith engines, hydraulic transmission and a 2+2 'express' style interior. It was later rebuilt to standard Class 150/0 configuration and ran alongside its sister in the West Midlands for many years.

Alongside the '150/0s', BR also tested a pair of three-car DMUs built by Metro-Cammell in the mid- to late-1980s. The

Class 141-144 railbuses introduced from 1985 onwards. It too used Leyland National body panels, but featured much more substantial cabs, moving away from the 'bus on a wagon' look of earlier prototypes.

From September 1986, No. 140001 was based at Neville Hill in Leeds for local services in Yorkshire, but by 1994 it was out of use and was sold for preservation in 1995. It is now in working order at the Keith & Dufftown Railway in Scotland.

In 2018, the Class 142-144 'Pacers' developed from these railbuses will start to be retired after more than 30 years in service. Designed for a life of just 10 years they have, whether we like them or

not, played a huge part in maintaining rail services to many parts of the country when the alternative would have been closure and bus replacement.

Heavy DEMU

While the railbuses were designed to replace first generation DMUs on lighter duties, BR was also faced with a dire need for new diesel units for busier suburban and interurban lines. First generation DMUs from the late-1950s and early-1960s were rapidly coming to the end of their lives and were increasingly unreliable and decrepit.

Two schools of thought emerged in BR

ABOVE: The two Class 150/0 prototypes of 1984 formed the basis of a large family of second generation underfloor DMUs and are still in service today. In January 1985, No. 150002 leaves Buxton with a test run to Manchester. RAIL PHOTOPRINTS

two Class 151 sets had a radically different externally appearance to their BREL rivals, but were mechanically similar to No. 150001. Both sets had a Cummins 285hp engine under each car with 'hot shift' twin disc transmissions and Gmeinder final drives to one bogie per car. They worked alongside the '150s' from Derby for several years, most often on the Matlock branch.

After the awarding of the production contract to BREL, the non-standard '151s' were on borrowed time and they were withdrawn in 1989. Various schemes to revive them were mooted over the years, but they were finally scrapped at Crewe in 2004.

Nos. 150001/002 are still very much active with Great Western Railway, more than 30 years after they were introduced. The 'Sprinter' concept has proved to be extremely successful for BR and its successors and the Class 150s, 155/156s and 158/159s are still an important part of the national DMU fleet.

As well as the Class 15x 'Sprinter' family, the two BREL prototypes greatly influenced the later Class 165/166 Networker Turbo DMUs which, in turn, were the basis of the post-privatisation ADtranz/ Bombardier Turbostar units. Hundreds of diesel railcars in service today can trace their origins back to those prototype railcars of the early 20th century. ●

ABOVE: In competition with the '150s' were Metro-Cammell angular Class 151s. All four prototype sets were based at Derby for comparative tests in the mid-1980s. CHRIS MILNER

In 1921 Scottish engineer George Bennie proposed a suspended high-speed monorail powered by a propeller. A demonstration line was eventually built over an LNER goods line at Milngavie, north of Glasgow, in 1929. Test and publicity runs commenced in July 1930, creating interest around the world but, in the long run, no firm orders. Ambitious schemes for a London-Paris/Brussels route, and a line running at up to 200mph across the Sahara Desert and the Middle East were later proposed.

ABOVE: A works portrait of one of the Lartigue system 0-3-0 locomotives built by Hunslet of Leeds for the Listowel & Ballybunion Railway in Ireland. ROBERT HUMM COLLECTION

Monorail!

Using just a single rail or beam, monorails have long been promoted as a cheaper way to build public and industrial railways in difficult terrain.

Often thought of as modern development, the first monorail was actually proposed in 1820 by Ivan Elmanov in Russia. For as long as railways have been around, engineers and inventors have been proposing single-rail alternatives to conventional railways, either to reduce construction costs or reach locations not possible with two rails.

The first British monorail was a horse-drawn system patented by Henry Palmer in 1821 and employed at Deptford dockyard in south-east London. Another short line was built for moving stone from a quarry

near Cheshunt in Hertfordshire to the River Lea and was not just the first monorail in the world to carry passengers but also the first railway in Hertfordshire.

Various schemes were proposed throughout the 19th century, but the city of Wuppertal in Germany was the first to introduce a commercial monorail line in 1901-03. The Wuppertal Schwebebahn is a suspended monorail running for more than eight miles through the city at a height of around 40ft. In many places the line is above the winding River Wupper or city streets. Still thriving today, it has 20 stations and carries

more than 25 million passengers a year.

Around the turn of the century, other monorail schemes were developed for military and industrial use, including a gyroscopically balanced vehicle running on a single rail. The Brennan gyroscopic monorail was tested by the War Department and demonstrated at the Japan-British Exhibition of 1910 but work was abandoned soon after.

However, probably the best-known monorail system of the period was designed by French engineer Charles Lartigue and developed from Palmer's horse-drawn scheme. Intended for use in the desert or

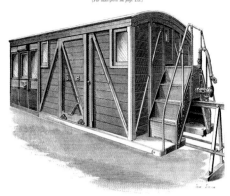

ROLLING STOCK, LISTOWEL AND BALLYBUNION RAILWAY.
(For description see page 175.)

ABOVE: Sketches of Listowel & Ballybunion Railway passenger vehicles, showing the awkward pannier design and the steps required to cross the elevated rail. ROBERT HUMM COLLECTION

ABOVE: The Wuppertal Schwebebahn (suspended railway) in western Germany was the first commercially successful monorail and continues to be an important part of the city's public transport system today. BEN JONES

ERECTED OVER
L·N·E·R LINE—
MILNGAVIE STATION
(NEAR GLASGOW)

Swift
Safe
Sure

THE GEORGE BENNIE
RAILPLANE SYSTEM OF TRANSPORT

ABOVE: Contemporary postcard showing the Bennie Railplane test track at Milngavie in Glasgow. ROBERT HUMM COLLECTION

across similar unstable, rolling terrain, his most famous commercial line was actually constructed in Ireland in 1888. The infamous 9¼ mile Listowel & Ballybunion Railway in Co. Kerry used Lartigue's system of a load-bearing single rail and two lower, external rails for balance, with all three carried on triangular 'A' frame steel trestles that could be assembled, installed and moved quickly when necessary. Other lines were built in France and across the Algerian desert, the latter using mules to pull pannier-style wagons.

However, the L&BR was the first monorail to use steam locomotives, and Hunslet of Leeds built several twin-boilered 0-3-0 machines for the line. These hauled trains of specially constructed passenger coaches and goods wagons which straddled the centre rail, much like the panniers carried by camels – Lartigue's original inspiration for the system.

Although construction costs were much lower than a conventional railway, the Lartigue system had significant drawbacks, not least the need to evenly balance all loads, the difficulty of crossing roads on the level (drawbridge style bridges were built at certain locations), pointwork and overall stability.

The line closed in 1924 after sustaining damage during the Irish Civil War and never reopened. Apart from a few sections of rail dumped in the peat, everything was scrapped. A high-speed Lartigue monorail between Liverpool and Manchester was proposed in 1901, although like most of the schemes around the world nothing came of it.

Bennie Railplane

In 1921 Scottish engineer George Bennie revived the idea of a suspended high-speed monorail powered by a propeller, which had first been mooted in the USA around three decades before. An initial proposal for a demonstration line to the British Empire Exhibition at Wembley in 1924 did not proceed beyond the planning stage, but a demonstration line was eventually built over an LNER goods line at Milngavie, north of Glasgow, in 1929.

Test and publicity runs commenced in July 1930, creating interest around the world but, in the long run, no firm orders. Ambitious schemes for a London-Paris/Brussels route, and a line running at up to 200mph across the Sahara Desert and the Middle East were proposed.

By 1936, Bennie had parted company with the Railplane board and was declared bankrupt the following year. However, he continued to promote various Railplane schemes until his death in 1957.

Remarkably, the steel structures of the Milngavie test track were not dismantled until 1956, despite being disused since before the Second World War.

By the second half of the 20th century, ▶

OVERSEAS RAILWAYS, A Railway Gazette Publication   165

GEORGE BENNIE AIRSPEED RAILPLANE
SWIFT . . . SAFE . . . SURE
200 MILES PER HOUR
THE TRANSPORT SOLUTION TO THE DESERT

500 miles across shifting sands in Three hours!

THE ESSENTIAL LINK BETWEEN TOWNS AND AIRPORTS
Designed to carry PASSENGERS—MAILS—PERISHABLE GOODS.
The speed of G.B.A.R. is 200 m.p.h., cruising 160 m.p.h., the carrying
capacity of each car is 50 passengers, cars can be despatched every
minute. Total carrying capacity for one hour is 3,000 passengers.
Maintenance is one-third of surface railway.

COST OF CONSTRUCTION (Prestressed Concrete and Aluminium)
ONE-THIRD OF A SURFACE RAILWAY
ONE-QUARTER of an ARTERIAL ROAD of the SAME LENGTH

Enquiries to:
GEORGE BENNIE AIRSPEED RAILWAY LIMITED
(All patents held by George Bennie)

Glasgow Address : 124 ST. VINCENT STREET, C.2 · London Address : 2 MUSEUM MANSIONS, W.C.1

ABOVE: A 1950s advertisement promoting George Bennie's proposal to build Railplane routes across the deserts of Africa and the Middle East. ROBERT HUMM COLLECTION

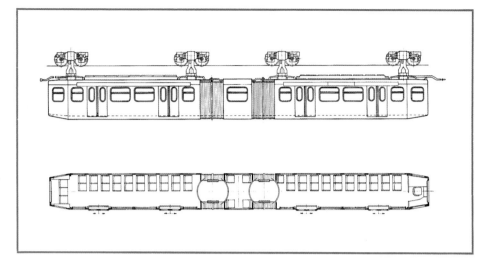

ABOVE: General arrangement diagram of the previous generation of MAN monorail trains for Wuppertal. ROBERT HUMM COLLECTION

monorails had moved towards using larger concrete beam or girder-based track, with vehicles supported by one set of wheels and guided by another. In the 1950s, a 40% scale prototype of a system designed to run at up to 200mph was built in Germany.

However, most lines that were built tended to be novelty lines for theme parks or short-distance people movers for airports and holiday resorts. These included the famous lines at Disneyland and Walt Disney World and in Las Vegas in the USA. Monorails were promoted as futuristic technology but generally failed to attract any interest as conventional transport systems.

However, a number of mass transit monorails have been constructed in cities around the world since the 1980s – most notably in Japan. Tokyo's monorail carries around 127,000 passengers per day and has served over 1.5 billion passengers since 1964. Recent additions include a wide-bodied mass transit system in Chongqing in China equivalent capacity to a heavy rail line – now the busiest in the world – and the Bombardier Innovia monorail metro system in the Brazilian city of Sao Paulo (pictured). The 14.9-mile guideway has 17 stations, 54 trains and a passenger capacity of 40,000 commuters per hour in each direction. Bombardier has also sold the Innovia system to Riyadh in Saudi Arabia. ●

ABOVE: Bombardier's modern Innovia monorail uses a broad concrete beam to guide trains powered by rubber tyres. The technology has been sold to Sao Paulo and Riyadh so far. RAILWAY MAGAZINE ARCHIVE

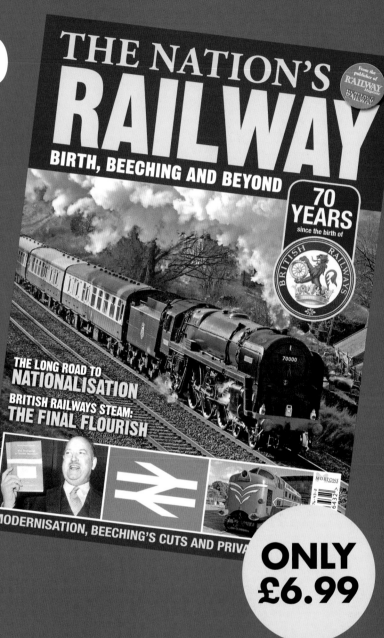

The Jet Age

When the pioneering main line diesels of the 1940s struggled to match the power output of larger steam locomotives, new jet engine technology seemed to offer a powerful alternative and various prototypes were built to test it.

ABOVE: Like many experimental locomotives testing new equipment, No. 18000 experienced many problems and failures in service and spent long periods at Swindon Works. On February 16, 1950 it was in the works for attention, offering quite a contrast to the other locomotives on site. COLOUR-RAIL

BR's Early Gas Turbines

Although diesel power was starting to prove itself as a viable alternative to steam traction before the outbreak of the Second World War, no single unit locomotive of the time could match the power of large main line locomotives.

Where a GWR 'King' 4-6-0 in 'good nick' could deliver around 2,500hp to the rails, and the LMS 'Princess Coronations' were capable of more than 3,000hp, the LMS/LMR and Southern Region diesel prototypes (Nos. 10000/01 and 10201/202) could only manage 1,600hp, reducing to around 1,300hp at the rails after transmission losses. Multiple working equipment

meant that one crew could drive two locomotives on heavier trains but this was an expensive solution and the search was soon under way for more power.

Rather than developing its own diesels, the Great Western Railway (GWR) looked to gas turbine power, ordering a prototype locomotive from Swiss company Brown Boveri in 1946.

Delays in construction and foreign currency shortages meant that the locomotive was not delivered until after Nationalisation, the project being inherited by British Railways Western Region when the finished machine was delivered in 1949.

No. 18000 was powered by a Brown

Boveri industrial gas turbine rated at 2,500hp and designed to run on cheap heavy fuel oil. The GWR selected this fuel rather than more expensive light oil as, at the time, it was in the process of converting many of its steam locomotives from coal to heavy oil firing.

To achieve better fuel economy it was fitted with a heat exchanger to recover waste heat from the exhaust. The pre-heated air entered a large, vertical, combustion chamber where the fuel was injected and burned. However, No. 18000 was notoriously heavy on fuel, a characteristic shared with many other gas turbine locomotives. Jet engines are at their most efficient when running at full power for long periods, something not possible on the railway, even on long-distance express work.

Running on six axle bogies with four traction motors arranged as an A1A-A1A, the locomotive had a maximum speed of 90mph and weighed 115 tons. For low-speed shunting and light engine moves, an auxiliary diesel engine was fitted. This proved particularly useful in and around London Paddington where the noise and fumes of the main engine prompted complaints from residents and passengers.

Like many experimental locomotives testing new equipment, No. 18000 experienced many problems and failures in service. Ash from the heavy oil damaged the turbine blades, and the combustion chamber liner required frequent replacement due to fire damage. The electrical control systems were complex for the time and gave much trouble while maintenance of the sensitive electrics in filthy steam depots created more problems. When one of the traction motors failed, it was simply isolated, leaving No. 18000 to limp on at reduced power with just three motors.

On its day, the locomotive showed itself to be capable of meeting the WR's expectations and saw sporadic use on revenue earning trains between Paddington, Bristol and the West of England. It even gained the nickname 'Kerosene Castle'.

However, a combination of heavy fuel consumption, poor reliability and a lack of suitable operations to achieve the necessary efficiency eventually led to No. 18000 being set aside after long periods out of traffic.

ABOVE: On May 23, 1953 No. 18000 and its Metrovick rival No. 18100 (left) peep out from Swindon Works 'A Shop' giving a rare opportunity to see the two gas turbines together. RAIL PHOTOPRINTS

It was officially withdrawn in December 1960 and stored at Swindon Works until 1964, when a strange turn of events led to a second life for this experimental locomotive.

No. 18000 was acquired by the International Union of Railways (UIC) and modified for tests examining the wheel/rail interface, during which it worked in Switzerland and Austria. No longer gas turbine powered, it was used as a hauled vehicle, working with various types of electric locomotive.

By 1975 it was resident at the UIC's Vienna Arsenal test centre, displayed outside the Mechanical Engineering test building, where it remained until the early-1990s.

However, many British enthusiasts recognised the significance of the locomotive and pressure increased to return it to the UK. In 1994 it returned, sponsored by BR's Railfreight Distribution sector, and went to Sheffield's Tinsley depot for external restoration.

ABOVE: On its day, No. 18000 showed itself to be capable of meeting the WR's expectations and saw sporadic use on revenue earning trains between Paddington, Bristol (pictured) and the West of England. It even gained the nickname 'Kerosene Castle'. COLOUR-RAIL

ABOVE: Just five months old and recently accepted for revenue earning service by the WR, No. 18100 pauses at Warwick on April 1, 1952. COLOUR-RAIL

Since then this tenacious survivor, now largely empty inside, has been resident at Crewe Heritage Centre, Barrow Hill and Didcot Railway Centre, where it is currently on display. It is now owned by the Pete Waterman Trust.

18100: The British Challenger

While the GWR went to Switzerland for No. 18000, it also wanted to build its own gas turbine prototype to compare with the Swiss machine. In 1946, the company agreed to work with Metropolitan-Vickers (MV) to produce a home-grown locomotive powered by a 3,500hp gas turbine running at 7,000rpm. Unlike No. 18000 it would run on lighter paraffin or pool gas oil, rather than the heavy fuel oil that had caused problems with the Swiss locomotive.

The gas turbine was of a type which would now be called a turboshaft engine but it differed from modern engines in having only one turbine to drive both the compressor and the output shaft. It was based on contemporary jet aircraft practice and had six horizontal combustion chambers spaced radially around the turbine shaft and no heat exchanger.

A twin cab, Co-Co locomotive was proposed, with a maximum speed of 90mph and capable of producing its maximum power output of 3,150hp at 75mph. The

GWR's requirement was for the locomotive to haul a 650t train at 81mph on level track, dropping to 43mph on a 1-in-100 gradient and 24mph on 1-in-50.

The GWR and MV agreed to share the costs of developing, building and modifying the prototype, with the GWR paying a further 25% to acquire it if the trials were a success.

However, the GWR found itself unable to fulfil its part of the agreement and MV was forced to find another contractor to assemble the mechanical parts of the locomotive. This included the controversial bogies which were the subject of some disagreement between MV and British Railways in 1948. Development continued throughout the late-1940s, with the GWR becoming British Railways Western Region in January 1948.

The completed No. 18100 was finally delivered to Swindon in December 1951, being hauled by rail from MV's Trafford Park works in Manchester via Crewe, Wellington and Wolverhampton and Banbury. On arrival it was found to be considerably heavier than the agreed 120 tons, weighing in at 129.5t. However, even at this weight, the axleload was less than a GWR 'King' 4-6-0 and without the 'hammer blow' of steam locomotives.

Running tests began on December 19, 1951 with short runs within the works

before a first main line run, to Stoke Gifford near Bristol on January 3, 1952.

Other test runs included hauling a 12-coach train from Swindon to Plymouth over the steep Devon banks in March 1952, increasing to a weighty 18 coaches and including challenging restarts on the 1-in-42 of Hemerdon Bank.

Main line tests continued until April, when No. 18100 was given its first outing on a timetabled passenger train. It was accepted by the WR's motive power department two weeks later. However, it didn't take long for the WR to realise that the gas turbine was a thirsty form of power for railway locomotives – an average of 3.6 gallons per mile was reported. An additional fuel tank was installed during a visit to Swindon Works in September/October 1952.

That said, records indicate that the MV power unit performed well in service and many of the recorded failures were caused by other mechanical and electrical components, including the control system and sticking relays. No. 18100 averaged around 3,000 miles between failures in 1952 – although not all of its 19 failures could be blamed on the machine itself. At the time there was very little experience of such modern technology on the railway and few staff were trained to deal with it. Equally, with just one locomotive available,

ABOVE: An almost new No. 18100 stands outside the Metropolitan-Vickers works at Trafford Park in Manchester in 1952. COLOUR-RAIL

the operating department could not create a diagram which made the most of its superior power and speed, so the promised efficiencies were difficult to prove.

However, problems continued with the bogies, which experienced cracked frames, and a broken spring in September 1953 required another visit to Swindon Works. While the spring was repaired, and No. 18100 ran a few more light engine tests in October/November of that year, it never hauled another passenger train.

In December 1953 it was sent back to MV's Dukinfield works for conversion to heavy oil firing (despite the reservations of various parties about its suitability as a fuel) and other modifications but these

never took place. In 1957, BR cancelled the project and instead ordered the conversion of No. 18100 into a prototype electric locomotive for use on the London Midland Region's 25kV AC pilot scheme on the Styal Loop near Manchester. As No. E1000 (later E2001), it played a brief role in the development of high-voltage AC electrification, which was quickly adopted as the UK standard in the late-1950s.

MV rebuilt the locomotive in 1958 as a 2,500hp A1A-A1A electric, weighing 109t, by removing the middle traction motor on each bogie. The work was done at the company's Stockton-on-Tees works and including fitting new electrical equipment, a Stone-Faiveley pantograph, Brown-Boveri

circuit braker and mercury arc rectifier units. It was also converted from WR right-hand drive to left-hand drive, with work being completed in October 1958.

However, No. 18100's second experimental career was short-lived. After the first production BR 'AL1' electrics were delivered in 1959, No. E2001 was again redundant and it was stored in late-1961. It was then stored at various locations, including on the closed ex-Great Central Railway London Extension near Akeman Street in Buckinghamshire. Official withdrawal took place in April 1968, but it was not scrapped until November 1972, when it finally succumbed at Cashmore's Great Bridge yard in the West Midlands. ●

ABOVE: In 1957, BR cancelled the project and instead ordered the conversion of No. 18100 into prototype electric locomotive E2001. By 1959, it was again redundant and stored at various locations, including on the closed ex-Great Central Railway London Extension near Akeman Street in Buckinghamshire where it was used for wind resistance testing in 1968. On January 25, 1970 it was captured dumped at Westcott, near Quinton Road. RAIL PHOTOPRINTS

ABOVE: **Official works portrait of GT3.** RAILWAY MAGAZINE ARCHIVE

GT3: EE's Brave Experiment

Conceived just after the Second World War, but not built until the late-1950s, English Electric's GT3 was Britain's last great experiment in producing a gas turbine-powered locomotive.

More closely resembling a steam locomotive than any modern form of traction, the origins of English Electric's Gas Turbine 3 (GT3) lay in the early-1950s. However, by the time it was completed in 1961, experiments with BR's first two gas turbine locomotives, Nos. 18000 and 18100, had already been terminated.

GT3 was built as a demonstrator at EE's Vulcan Foundry between 1958 and 1961 to a design by J.O.P. Hughes. The unique concept combined a 4-6-0 locomotive chassis similar to a BR Standard 5MT and

a tender built to carry kerosene fuel for the gas turbine and the steam heating boiler.

An EM27L gas turbine of 2,700hp was installed on the strengthened loco chassis, which was designed to cope with the greater torque of the power unit. GT3 weighed 123.5 tons and had a maximum design speed of 90mph.

Hughes' idea was to make the mechanical aspects of the locomotive and transmission as simple as possible, to deliver easier maintenance, high availability, a low power-to-weight ratio and the ability to burn low-grade fuel, overcoming the inherent

disadvantages of gas turbines for railway use – namely their high fuel consumption when running at less than full power.

The simple mechanical transmission featured one final drive mounted directly on to one coupled axle of the rigid wheelbase, avoiding any complexities from flexible drives to axles carried on bogies. The power unit was mounted vertically above the rear pair of bogie wheels, connected to the gearbox powering the middle driving axle.

Careful design allowed the various components to be neatly accommodated within the constraints of the British

ABOVE: A remarkable shot of GT3 under construction at EE's Vulcan Foundry alongside electric locomotives for export to South Africa. RAILWAY MAGAZINE ARCHIVE

loading gauge, and resulted in relatively few failures during GT3's running tests on BR main lines. Contemporary reports highlight the superb fit and finish of the locomotive, including its plush-carpeted cab, fine detailing and striking gloss red oxide paintwork with yellow/black lining.

By basing the new locomotive's transmission on that of Stanier's 'Turbomotive', it was a given that the drive of the English Electric machine would be direct through large coupled wheels in the manner of a steam locomotive. One such design produced featured a centre-cab 4-8-4, an illustration of which resides at the National Railway Museum showing the locomotive to be named *Britannic* and numbered 19000.

However, it was felt economies could be made if a traditional steam loco layout was adopted instead for the prototype only, allowing fuel, water and a train heating boiler to be carried in a separate tender. At this time BR was still building the 'Standard' classes and steam was still prevalent, so the availability of turning facilities was of no real concern. Consequently a generic 4-6-0 wheel arrangement was selected, a rather futuristic illustration appearing of a locomotive named *Lord of the Isles*.

It has been suggested over the years that the frames of a GWR 'Castle', an LMS 'Black Five' or a BR '5MT' were considered or used as the basis of the locomotive, but apart from sharing the 4-6-0 configuration, the main frames were in fact totally unique. If the locomotive was to have anything like the

required adhesion, it would be necessary for it to carry 60 tons over the three driving axles, with couple wheels of 5ft 9in diameter. The EM27A unit only weighed in at 15 tons and the transmission at 20 tons, so the main frames were made from 2½in plate in order to provide additional ballast.

Although still far from complete, the locomotive was booked to undergo evaluation at the Rugby Testing Station, but there remains some confusion as to

when these first tests were carried out. Some sources give the precise dates as July 27, 1957 to January 31, 1958, while a more common belief is that the test began in January 1959; the locomotive remaining at Rugby for 11 months.

The locomotive as it emerged from the Vulcan Foundry was 'naked', being devoid of body casing, cab or tender. The chassis looked for all the world like it had come from an inside-cylinder steam loco,

ABOVE: Some of the locomotive's early tests were undertaken before construction had been completed and GT3 was towed to Rugby at low speed in this 'naked' form. RAILWAY MAGAZINE ARCHIVE

large exhaust heat exchanger, all of which sat atop of the turbine shaft. Owing to the high temperatures generated when running, a high pressure lubrication system was installed with mechanical pumps doing the work. These only operated when the turbine was in motion so a second set of electric pumps had to be fitted to cover the pre-ignition and post-shut down periods to ensure that lubrication was maintained. To power these auxiliary pumps, and also to turn the turbine when starting, two large banks of batteries were installed on either side of the locomotive above the driving wheels at running plate level.

Towing the locomotive to Rugby was not without its problems. As a precaution a maximum speed of 15mph was adhered to, but just 13 miles from starting out the gearbox bearings failed and the locomotive had to return to Newton-le-Willows. Once the damage was repaired the journey was tried again, this time with the locomotive's coupling rods removed and the centre driving axle jacked up. It arrived without further mishap, and subsequently this method of moving the dead locomotive was always employed over long distances.

The English Electric machine became the first non-steam locomotive to use the Rugby facility, requiring special modifications to be made to the smoke hoods to deal with the high thermal output from the exhaust grilles. Unfortunately early tests with the locomotive on the dynamometer test rollers revealed lubrication and oil leakage problems, resulting in the gearbox primary shaft bearings reaching 100°C when running at 90mph. Consequently the engine unit had to be removed and returned to Whetstone for attention. When it was eventually refitted, an extensive range of tests was completed

ABOVE: In 1959, GT3 was the first non-steam locomotive to be tested on the rolling road at BR's Rugby Test Station. It remained on site for 11 months. RAILWAY MAGAZINE ARCHIVE

featuring heavy section coupling rods with roller bearings on the cranks, plus an outside framed bogie. Above the traditional running plate level, the EM27L was visible for all to see, showing the relatively compact nature of the gas turbine. At the front, in the space typically occupied by the smokebox, were two large banks of air filters (32 each side) which utilised specially developed washable convoluted paper filter elements. In the 'smokebox door' position

was an access door, beneath which was a fan that was mounted on the end of the turbine shaft that ran the length of the locomotive. Final drive from this shaft was to the centre set of driving wheels; a flexible arrangement allowing vertical movement of the wheelset and gearbox. This itself was interlocked, thereby preventing any gear changes while the locomotive was in motion.

Behind the air filters sat the combustion chambers, to the rear of which was the

ABOVE: Now 'fully clothed', GT3 ran tests over various BR lines in 1961/62 and proved to be a powerful, if fuel hungry, machine. RAIL PHOTOPRINTS

ABOVE: Some of GT3's most impressive outings were on the northern section of the West Coast Main Line, where performance was said to be akin to a Stanier 'Duchess' on the climb to Shap summit. The gas turbine passes Dillicar troughs with a train of ex-LMS stock in tow. COLOUR-RAIL

with satisfactory results. A maximum of 2,000hp was achieved at the wheel rims when running at 55mph, with a top speed of 97mph being attained.

These encouraging figures prompted further loaded tests to be undertaken on a lightly laid test track at Rugby. For these an adapted tanker wagon was employed to carry fuel as the locomotive's tender was still being completed at the Vulcan Foundry. It must have presented an incongruous sight to anyone who witnessed it as the 'alien' locomotive hauled a pair of dead Stanier '8F' 2-8-0s up the 1-in-44 on a 5½ chain curve and from a standing start.

Satisfied with the test results, the engine unit was again removed and sent for testing at Whetstone while work to complete the locomotive was undertaken at Newton-le-Willows.

Disappointingly for the project team, BR's interest in the possibilities of the gas turbine appeared to be waning. Even as the new locomotive entered the paintshop at the end of 1960, BR withdrew No. 18000 (two years after the withdrawal of No. 18100) and has apparently put its faith in diesel-hydraulics on the Western Region.

Even English Electric seemed to be taking a huge gamble in continuing the project, having introduced its D20/1s (Class 40s) in 1958 and was well advanced with the construction of the production 'Deltics' and what would later become the Class 37s and Class 83s. BR's final steam locomotive had emerged from Swindon works earlier that year, and it was a sure bet that diesel and electric power was here to stay.

After testing on the rolling road at BR's Rugby test centre, the locomotive was unleashed on the main line, running trials on the former Great Central London Extension south of Leicester and on the West Coast Main Line between Crewe and Carlisle. Railway writer and engineer O.S.

Nock recorded some exceptional work by GT3 on the latter route, with the climb from Tebay to Shap summit being despatched in 6¼ minutes with 12 coaches in tow, despite only working at seven-eighths of full power. In another test, GT3 accelerated from a stand to 70mph in around seven minutes on level track with a train weighing 638t; Bulleid diesel No. 10202, rated at 1,600hp, could do the same but only with a trailing load of 399t. On another occasion, GT3 dismissed the 30.5 uphill miles from Carlisle Upperby to Shap in 42 minutes, against a schedule of 52 minutes, with 458t in tow – a performance more akin to a Stanier 'Duchess' 4-6-2 in good fettle.

During GT3's trials over the Great Central Main Line, English Electric received considerable interest in the project from both Union Pacific and Polish State Railways, the latter sending representatives over to see the locomotive in action. BR also was impressed with the performances, prompting EE to push on with the WCML tests, which were completed in early 1962. Having run for approximately 500 hours and having covered a total of 11,000 miles, GT3 returned to Newton-le-Willows, the intention being to fit a spare gas turbine and prepare the locomotive for revenue-earning service. The hope was that after a period of two or three years, small orders for locomotives based on the GT3 technology would follow.

However, by the time GT3 was ready, English Electric was deeply engaged in constructing diesel-electric locomotives of several types for BR and the project was not followed up. In fact, while GT3 was on test, BR had already selected the Brush Type 4 Co-Co (Class 47) as its new standard high-power Type 4, despite reservations in certain quarters about whether 2,750hp was enough for future requirements.

Despite its potential, GT3 had a number

of inherent problems, not least the steam locomotive style design, which required turntables at each end of any route it worked – something being eliminated as diesel traction took over. The ten-year delay between the original idea and completion of the prototype doomed it to irrelevance before it had turned a wheel, as BR was fully committed to diesel traction by 1961.

For four years GT3 sat under a tarpaulin in the yard at the Vulcan Foundry, quietly forgotten, until a curious journalist happened to have a peek under the wraps during an English Electric press event. The resulting media storm was probably the catalyst for EE finally deciding to dispose of the locomotive, and in early 1966 it was dragged into the works for the removal of the EM27L power plant and other fittings. That February GT3 suffered the final insult as '4MT' 4-6-0 No. 75032 arrived to drag the locomotive to Thomas Ward's scrapyard in Salford, where it was later cut up.

Some 20 years after the concept of GT3 was drawn up, and after just two years of operation, the locomotive was scrapped – English Electric receiving just £600 for its remains. It has been argued that GT3 arrived too late, and had it got off the drawing board earlier it might have stood a greater chance of success. Certainly there was scope for potentially using the technology to give a second life to redundant steam loco frames or, as originally planned, to create a class of double-ended locomotives as a viable alternative to diesel traction. Yet such arguments are merely speculation, and as author Kevin Robertson notes in his book 'The Great Western Gas Turbines: A Myth Exposed' – "If GT3 came too late, it is a wonder that it was ever built at all."

• With thanks to Gary Boyd-Hope for much of the additional information contained in this article. ●

Ahead of the Curve

BR's answer to increasing competition from air and road travel was the Advanced Passenger Train – pushing the limits of rail and aerospace technology to run faster over existing lines.

ABOVE: Much of APT-E's early testing took place on the BR test track at Old Dalby. It was the world's first self-propelled active tilting train and the first to use computer designed wheelsets and active suspension to eliminate hunting. RAILWAY MAGAZINE ARCHIVE

It was sleek, secretive and fast, with technologies imported from previously unknown sources. No, not a US spy plane from the Cold War, but BR's secret weapon in the fight against road and air transport in the late-1960s and early-1970s.

The Advanced Passenger Train (APT) concept was first mooted in the early-1960s and over the next 20 years developed from an idea to a working prototype and eventually pre-series trains that BR hoped would help it to win passengers back from the motorways and airlines. It's a fascinating story, packed with imagination, intrigue, triumph and, ultimately, disappointment.

Fifteen years after its creation, British Railways was in financial turmoil and facing ever-growing competition from air travel and mass car ownership. Around the same time, BR's research, development and engineering teams were brought together as the new Railway Technical Centre (RTC) which opened in Derby in 1964. Hundreds of highly qualified engineers and technicians from various railway departments and recruited from other sectors, most notably the aerospace industry, made it a hothouse for new ideas.

Railways across Europe were suffering similar problems to BR, but where major investments had been made in electrification and shorter journey times, it was found that passengers could be won back in droves. In Britain, the best example was on the West Coast Main Line, where electrification had led to what became known as the 'sparks effect'. It was claimed that a reduction of 10% in journey times could result in a 10% increase in revenue – an excellent basis on which to lobby the government for investment in new trains.

Elsewhere in the world, new and expensively realigned railways were planned and built, but in the UK any reduction in journey times would have to be won from existing lines dating back to the 19th century. The BR marketing team's target of 150mph would be no mean feat on lines such as the WCML, where the existing maximum of 100mph could only be achieved

ABOVE: A 1969 vision of how BR's Advanced Passenger Train might look. RAILWAY MAGAZINE ARCHIVE

in short bursts. An entirely new type of train was required – it became known as the Advanced Passenger Train (APT).

Tests around the world had proved that achieving higher speeds (125mph/200kph and above) safely required much more than installing huge amounts of power. Braking, interaction between the wheel and rail, aerodynamics, suspension systems, signalling and many other factors were investigated by the RTC over the next five years. The major breakthrough came in 1967 when a radical proposal for a high-speed train that tilted through curves, much like a motorcyclist, was revealed.

In 1969, development had progressed to the stage where it was deemed necessary to build a locomotive-hauled prototype train – known as APT-POP – to test the tilt systems and articulated bogies prior to commissioning a fully operational experimental APT set. This unusual open-framed and heavily instrumented train was hauled by conventional locomotives, including the RTC's own 'Clayton' Class 17.

APT-E development

Skipping forward to July 1972, APT-Experimental (APT-E) made its first tentative

venture on to the main line. Powered by four British Leyland gas turbines, giving a total of 2,400hp for the lightweight four-car train, the train's aerospace influence was unmistakable. Sleek aluminium bodies, unpainted but for a Rail blue bodyside band and yellow warning panels, and a radical streamlined shape made this quite unlike anything seen on British rails before.

Two driving cars housed the power units, sandwiching a pair of articulated trailers. Gas turbines were used because they were much lighter than diesel engines of the required power and much of the early testing would take place on

ABOVE: APT-E parked at the Railway Technical Centre in Derby in the early-1970s, where it was built and much of its development work took place. RAILWAY MAGAZINE ARCHIVE

ABOVE: On August 10, 1975 APT-E achieved a speed of 152.3mph while on test on the Western Region between Didcot and Swindon. COLOUR-RAIL

non-electrified lines. Chief among these was the former Midland Railway Melton Mowbray-Nottingham route, which was commandeered by the RTC for use as a dedicated test track after closure.

It was completed and handed over to the Research Division on July 8, 1970 but a number of improvements to the curves, especially at Upper Broughton and Folly Hall, were frequently carried out during the subsequent APT-E testing programme, in order to raise the speed limit.

A great deal of testing was carried out at Old Dalby in connection with the APT development programme using various vehicles including the open frame units known as POP train. This name was derived from the fact that there were two

ABOVE: To allow towing by locomotives with conventional buffing gear, APT-P's streamlined nose could be lifted, a feature that proved useful when the train failed or was being moved around for testing. RAIL PHOTOPRINTS

ABOVE: Although the experimental APT set was powered by gas turbines, the prototype and production trains were to be electric for use on the West Coast Main Line. APT-P No. 370002 poses on the curved approach to Preston station in October 1979. RAIL PHOTOPRINTS

stage of development – an electric APT that could also carry passengers.

APT-Prototype (APT-P) was unveiled to the public in June 1978 and three complete 14-car trains, organised into six identical half-sets numbered No. 370001-006, plus two spare cars, were built.

Two central motor cars, basically tilting locomotives without driving cabs, sat between 12 articulated trailer cars provided 8,000hp in total. For many years APT-P was the most powerful train ever to run in Britain, and that allowed it to beat APT-E's UK rail speed record in December 1979, setting a new maximum of 162.2mph. The record stood for 23 years until a shortened InterCity 225 set powered by No. 91010 just beat it with a 162.6mph dash down Stoke Bank in Lincolnshire. The Class 91s use traction equipment derived from the APT-P power cars!

After testing without passengers in 1978/79, APT-P was used in public service, albeit sporadically, on the West Coast Main Line (WCML) between 1980 and 1986. The awkward arrangement with power cars in the centre meant that passengers could not walk through the whole train, which was effectively split into two halves. Each half required its own staff and catering facilities, which increased costs and reduced flexibility.

APT-P soon proved itself capable of matching the original 150mph target set by BR's marketing team and was regularly run at up to its design speed of 155mph. In passenger service, 125mph was the normal maximum but its ability to run much more quickly than conventional trains through curves on the northern half of the WCML had the potential to slash journey times.

However, the sheer quantity of new technology contained with the trains, particularly systems such as the active tilt and hydrodynamic braking, meant that failures were common and the trains were often stopped for repairs or improvements.

At a time when BR was struggling for investment from the government, APT-P was an expensive programme that had been in progress for almost two decades without delivering the transformation it promised. Unfortunately, just as the APT engineering team seemed to be making real progress, the project was cancelled in 1986 and the trains were hastily despatched to C.F. Booth's yard in Rotherham for scrap. Famously, the destruction of most of the fleet was captured by a regional TV crew and beamed across the nation – a sad end for a concept that promised so much.

A few cars survive as static exhibits at Crewe Heritage Centre as a reminder of what could have been. Ironically, they are passed numerous times every hour by Italian-built Class 390 Virgin Pendolino tilting EMUs which use technology derived from the APT project and sold to FIAT for use in its Italian tilting trains. Since the early-2000s, the West Coast Main Line has benefited hugely from 125mph tilting EMUs, which it might have enjoyed a decade earlier if APT had been allowed to blossom. ●

power bogies surrounding an articulated trailer bogie (hence Power nil Power) and the whole formation was loco-hauled to test the tilt, bogies and suspension. This commenced running at Old Dalby in the autumn of 1971, although APT-E itself did not start running until September 1973 as it was 'blacked' by the drivers' union ASLEF for 12 months after its first run on the main line to Duffield.

The APT-E consisted of two driving power cars (PC1 and 2) and two trailer cars (TC1 and 2). The power cars were equipped with four 300 HP Leyland 350 gas turbines (and a fifth for auxiliary power supplies) and two GEC 253AY nose suspended traction motors on the leading bogies. Each vehicle was about 70ft long with articulated bogies between them.

It was the world's first self-propelled active tilting train and the first to use computer designed wheelsets and active suspension to eliminate hunting.

On August 10, 1975 APT-E achieved a speed of 152.3mph while on test on the Western Region. In January 1976 it ran at 143.6 miles per hour at Old Dalby, some achievement on a limited length line. It was withdrawn after it had completed its test programmes and on June 11, 1976 made its final journey to the NRM York where it now resides.

APT goes electric

Results gathered from the APT-E programme were enough to convince BR that it was time to invest in the next

The Sparks Effect

Electric trains are seen as the epitome of clean, modern and efficient rail traction, but they've been with us since the late-19th century, transforming underground, urban and inter-city railways in all their forms.

MORECAMBE (PROM)

As the forerunner of modern British AC electrification, the Midland Railway's Lancaster-Morecambe-Heysham scheme played a hugely significant role in the development of electric traction in this country. On August 17,1953 one of the former LNWR Siemens third-rail EMUs, rebuilt for 6,600V AC overhead operation, pauses at Lancaster (Green Ayre) with a service for Morecambe Promenade. RAILWAY MAGAZINE ARCHIVE

ABOVE: Urban railways were the first to benefit from electric traction, with the famous Liverpool Overhead Railway being a pioneer in many respects. No. 42 was one of the line's original wooden bodied sets, captured here around 1910. RAILWAY MAGAZINE ARCHIVE

While in the UK we consider electric trains to be a relatively modern development, the first electrically powered rail vehicle moved under its own power in Britain as early as 1842 – just 13 years after the legendary Rainhill Trials. Scottish scientist and inventor Robert Davison tested a rudimentary locomotive powered by electro-magnetism on the Edinburgh & Glasgow Railway in September 1842. This was 37 years before Werner von Siemens presented what is generally regarded as the world's first electric train. However, Siemens' little exhibition train of 1879 was indeed the first to employ electric motors powered by an external source – in this case 150V DC – and was therefore the direct forerunner of the electric trains we see today.

Over the next few years, Siemens went on to build the world's first electric tramway in Berlin (1881), the first electric trolleybus, mine locomotives and the first underground railway in mainland Europe – in Budapest.

In 1890, Britain's first underground electric railway, the 3.2-mile City & South London Railway was the world's first electric 'deep tube' line. Trains were powered by a 500V DC third-rail supply setting the pattern for the current London Underground network. Eventually the C&SLR was extended and became part of what is now LU's Northern Line.

However, even that pioneer is beaten by the world's oldest operating electric railway, Brighton's Volk's Electric Railway opened in August 1883. Built by inventor and engineer Magnus Volk, trains on the 2ft gauge railway were powered by a 2hp Otto gas engine driving a Siemens DC generator.

ABOVE: The North Eastern Railway was one of the first main line companies to adopt electric operation for suburban services. Its North Tyneside fleet of 1904 included a pair of Motor Parcels Vans, one of which survives as part of the National Collection. RAILWAY MAGAZINE ARCHIVE

Rebuilt to 2ft 8½ in gauge with larger and more powerful trains in 1883/84, it ran in this form along Brighton beach until the threat of enemy invasion forced its closure in 1940. Despite many setbacks, storm damage and two World Wars, the line continues to operate as a tourist attraction today.

Another British pioneer was the Liverpool Overhead Railway, which opened in 1893. The LOR was the world's first electric elevated railway, the first to use automatic signalling with colour light signals and the first use of Electric Multiple Unit (EMU) trains. It also had one of the first passenger escalators at a railway station. At its peak, more than 20m people a year used the 'Docker's Umbrella' as it was known locally, but sadly it fell into

disrepair after being damaged in the Second World War and eventually closed in 1956.

The Mersey Railway, also serving Liverpool and its suburbs, went over to electric operation on May 3, 1903, using electrical equipment imported from Westinghouse in the USA. Trains ran every three minutes under the River Mersey from Liverpool Central to Birkenhead Hamilton Square in a much cleaner environment than the steam trains used previously.

Urban Electrics

By the late-19th century, residents of the big cities of Europe and North America were becoming increasingly concerned about pollution from steam trains and electric traction appeared to provide a perfect solution – clean, modern and efficient, it was already being widely used for street-running trams, replacing horses and wildly unsuitable steam trams.

In Britain, electrification was viewed by main line railway companies as necessary defence against the new electric tram systems springing up in many towns and cities. In March 1904, the Lancashire & Yorkshire Railway's Liverpool-Southport line became the first outside the capital to 'go electric', using 625V DC third-rail EMUs. A fourth 'return' rail was positioned centrally between the two running rails. Additional trains were later built for this route, and for the Ormskirk route in 1913. Remarkably, a number of lightweight EMU sets were also built to provide through services from Southport and Aintree over the Liverpool Overhead Railway until 1914.

In contrast to the steam-hauled carriages they replaced, the four-car trains had airy open saloons and electric lighting. Importantly, they also reduced the journey time from 54 to 37 minutes.

The original Southport units were replaced by the LMS in the early-1940s, but the Ormskirk units survived until 1964.

An experimental electric locomotive, rebuilt from a 2-4-2 steam locomotive, was introduced in 1912 for goods traffic. It had four 150hp traction motors and could collect current from the third-rail on the main line or from overhead wires in Aintree and North Mersey yards. It was scrapped in 1919.

The LYR also experimented with overhead electric supply for suburban trains; in 1913 it converted a short branch from Bury to Holcombe Brook, north of Manchester to 3,600V DC operation. Equipment was provided by electric traction specialist Dick, Kerr of Preston, which had an eye on the export market.

The Manchester Victoria-Bury line was electrified using a unique 1,200V DC side-contact third-rail system in 1916. The original LYR trains were replaced by BR in 1959/60, but the non-standard third-rail supply system was retained. This arrangement continued until the line was converted for Metrolink light rail operation in 1991/92. In 1919, after a major fault with the power supply, the Holcombe Brook line was re-electrified at 1,200V DC to match its neighbour. The experimental 3,600V DC EMU was converted into Britain's first diesel-electric multiple unit (DEMU) by the LMS in 1927/28 (see page 52).

Tyneside Electrics

When the Newcastle electric tramway system opened in 1902, the local lines of the North Eastern Railway (NER) lost four million passengers – 40% of their 1901 total – almost overnight. Fortunately, the NER's directors foresaw this loss of traffic and chose to electrify the North Tyneside suburban lines as quickly as possible. A 600V DC third-rail system was deployed, using top contact collector shoes mounted on the bogies

ABOVE: An example of the Lancashire & Yorkshire Railway's Manchester-Bury line EMUs of 1916, seen at Bury Bolton Street in June 1959, shortly before the introduction of new BR EMUs. COLOUR-RAIL

ABOVE: The London Brighton & South Coast Railway was an early advocate of AC overhead electrification, marketed as 'The Elevated Electric', and wired much of its south London suburban network between 1909 and 1922. RAILWAY MAGAZINE ARCHIVE

of the electric vehicles. The first section between New Bridge Street and Benton took place on March 29, 1904, making it the second electric passenger service operated by a British main line railway company. The LYR's Southport-Liverpool services started just a week earlier.

The Tyneside system was fully operational by July 1904, and quickly regained much of the lost traffic. In fact, the Tyneside Electrics were so successful

that a further 35 vehicles had been added to the fleet by 1915 to cope with the additional passengers. The original NER wooden-planked electric trains continued in service until replaced by the LNER in 1937. However, electric operation was abandoned on the North Tyneside lines in 1967 and replaced by BR diesel railcars until the late-1970s, when the lines were closed for conversion to light rail standard as part of the Tyne & Wear Metro system. ▶

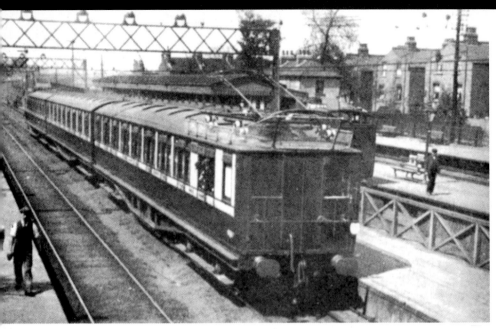

ABOVE: An LBSCR 'elevated electric' train calls at Wandsworth around 1909. RAILWAY MAGAZINE ARCHIVE

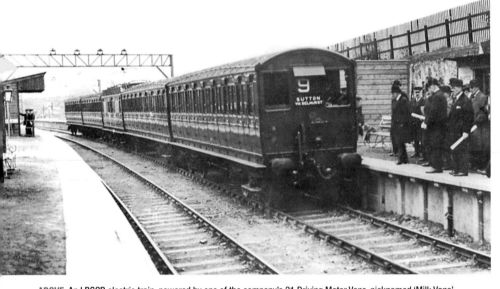

ABOVE: An LBSCR electric train, powered by one of the company's 21 Driving Motor Vans, nicknamed 'Milk Vans', sandwiched between four trailer coaches. These motor vans were built for the extension of AC electrification to Coulsdon North and Sutton. RAILWAY MAGAZINE ARCHIVE

ABOVE: An ex-LNWR EMU led by Driving Trailer Third M29024M heads away from Lancaster with a train for Morecambe Promenade. COLOUR-RAIL

AC Overhead

The Midland Railway also experimented with electric traction in the 1900s and chose its Lancaster (Green Ayre) to Morecambe and Heysham branch to conduct the trials. The route had previously been the site of unsuccessful steam railmotor operations.

Unlike previous electrification schemes, the MR selected a 6,600V, 25Hz alternating current (AC) overhead system; arguably the world's first 'modern' electric railway.

Electric trains started in 1908 using EMUs formed from a fleet of three Driving Motor (DM) cars and six Driving Trailers. The DMs had a cab at each end, allowing trains of one, two, or three cars to be formed.

The DMs were built at Derby Works, two with Siemens electrical equipment and the third with Westinghouse equipment. Of the six DTs, four were built new at Derby Works, and two others were converted from existing hauled stock.

The MR sets were finally withdrawn by British Railways in February 1951, after which steam-hauled trains worked the line. However, that only lasted until August 1953 when experimental electric traction returned in the form of BR 'AM1' units working at the new frequency of 6,600V 50Hz AC.

Although BR had continued with the LNER standard 1,500V DC overhead standard for its early electrification scheme on the Woodhead Route and Liverpool Street-Shenfield suburban line, high voltage AC was increasingly seen as more efficient. Various trials were conducted in mainland Europe with AC traction after the Second World War.

The power supply was fed through rectifiers and transformers to the DC traction motors of the 'AM1s', providing useful experience with this technology and eventually leading to the adoption of the 25kV AC 50Hz system for the West Coast Main Line electrification scheme from the late-1950s.

Far from being new trains, the 'AM1s' were 1952 rebuilds of ex-London & North Western Railway/Siemens Watford DC lines four-rail stock.

Each of the four electric units featured different electrical equipment, and although the original Midland electrification infrastructure was used in places, other sections were used for trials of BR's proposed standard electrification equipment. Outside the peak holiday season, there was little traffic on the route, and the ex-LNWR line to Morecambe provided an alternative diesel railcar service. From Lancaster Castle station, electric trains ran a short distance to the ex-MR Lancaster (Green Ayre) station, where they reversed and ran along the River Lune to Morecambe Promenade, reversing again to run to Heysham. It provided an ideal test line, and paved the way for BR's early 25kV AC EMU fleets, delivered from the late-1950s. The

'AM1s' were finally withdrawn when the line closed to passengers in April 1966.

Today, AC EMUs form the majority of trains on electrified lines away from the former Southern Region, ranging from 1970s Class 313-315 suburban types to 125mph tilting 'Pendolino' sets and the various new EMUs being delivered by Bombardier, Hitachi, Siemens, Stadler and CAF over the next three years.

South of the Thames

Railway companies serving south London and the city's rapidly expanding suburbs were also concerned about competition from electric tramways. In December 1909, the London Brighton & South Coast Railway (LBSCR) started its first electric operation between London Bridge and Victoria. Looking ahead to wider main line electrification, it adopted a 6,600V AC overhead system for its suburban lines, with electrical equipment supplied by AEG of Germany. Marketed as 'The Elevated Electric' it was an immediate success and electrification was extended from Victoria to Crystal Palace via Balham by May 1911 and from Peckham Rye to West Norwood in March 1912. The success of the system convinced the LBSCR to extend electric operation to all its London suburban lines in 1913, although the work was delayed by the First World War. By 1925 most of the LBSCR inner suburban lines were wired along with the routes to Coulsdon and Sutton and plans were in place for main line electrification to Brighton,

ABOVE: One of the last experimental BR EMUs was the Class 457 Networker development train, rebuilt from Class 210 prototype DEMU cars. It was used to test the new traction package and control equipment for the Class 365/465/466 EMUs introduced from the mid-1990s. COLOUR-RAIL

Eastbourne, Worthing, Newhaven, Seaford, Epsom and Oxted. However, the Grouping of 1923 put an end to these plans as the Southern Railway adopted the London & South Western Railway (LSWR) 750V DC third-rail system as its new standard. In 1926 the SR announced that all overhead electrified lines would be converted to third-rail and the final 6,600V AC overhead trains ran on September 29, 1929.

The two systems don't strictly fall into our experimental remit, but the LSWR system provided the basis for the Southern Railway's much wider third-rail electrification after 1923, which continues to be the standard for electric railways south of the Thames. Today, 750V DC third-rail stretches from Ramsgate and Dover to Weymouth, covering almost the entire suburban network south of the Thames, and even continuing around the North London Line. ●

ABOVE: BR's experiments with electric traction weren't limited to EMUs with external power supplies. In 1958, Derby Lightweight railcar Sc79998 was fitted with two Siemens-Schuckert traction motors and 216 lead-acid batteries for tests as a Battery Electric Railcar with Driving Trailer Sc79999. The unit worked until December 1966 on the Aberdeen-Ballater branch in north-east Scotland. COLOUR-RAIL

Britain's Only Double-Deck Trains

Just like today, the Southern Railway's suburban electric routes suffered from chronic overcrowding at peak times. Extending platforms to accommodate longer trains is hugely expensive in built-up areas, particularly in central London. Faced with an estimated £10m bill to extend platforms on the lines from Charing Cross/Cannon Street to Dartford, SR Chief Mechanical Engineer O.V.S. Bulleid suggested double-deck trains to increase capacity without lengthening trains.

Full scale wooden mock-ups were built under conditions of strict secrecy at Lancing Works in 1948/49 to test Bulleid's design. Two prototype sets, Nos. 4001 and 4002, were built at Lancing (underframes) and Eastleigh (bodyshells), each formed of two Driving Motor Brake Second and two Trailer Second cars.

The units had what would become the standard SR traction package of EE507 motors with electro-pneumatic control gear, although their experimental Westinghouse EP brakes meant they were not compatible with other classes. The motor bogies had non-standard 8ft frames, 3ft diameter wheels – 2in smaller than standard. Top speed was 75mph.

Initial trials took place between Brighton and Haywards Heath, but various problems meant that both sets returned to works for extensive modifications. The extra 4.5in height of the '4-DD' sets meant that they were subject to severe route restrictions. Despite this, they entered service from Slade Green depot near Dartford on November 1, 1949.

Although called 'double-deck' trains, they were not twin-floor vehicles in the sense of a double-deck bus. Each compartment could seat 11 passengers, six on one side and five on the other with the space there occupied by steps to the upper compartment.

The upper level also had two tip-up seats situated where the door would normally be. Additional internal space was won within the loading gauge by having vertical bodysides, smaller wheels and less padding in the seats.

The DMBS cars seated 120 while the intermediate TS cars seated 156. One 12-seat central compartment on the lower level had no access to the upper deck. The full eight-car train could carry 1,104 seated passengers (compared to 772 in a standard eight-car EMU),

plus standees, but the small number of doors extended dwell times at stations by as much as 36% – unacceptable on routes with a train every couple of minutes. Passengers also tended to avoid going upstairs, preferring to stand in lower deck compartments. Seated passengers had less space and as the upper compartments had no opening windows they could become very warm on hot days.

As early January 1951 *The Railway Magazine* reported that The Railway Executive had decided that the extra capacity offered by the '4-DD' design was outweighed by the additional operational complexities it introduced and the reduced comfort for passengers. Despite this, the two '4-DD' sets remained in traffic until October 1, 1971, spending more than 20 years plying back and forth between Charing Cross and Dartford.

Britain's restricted loading gauge still precludes the introduction of double-deck trains on the classic network, although they have been mooted as a possibility for the proposed High Speed 2 (HS2) 'captive' trains that will work the new Euston-Birmingham-Manchester/Leeds routes from 2033. ●

ABOVE: Two prototype double-deck EMUs worked on the Southern Region's Charing Cross-Dartford route from 1949 until October 1971. Shortly before withdrawal, No. 4902 leads a Dartford working at Charing Cross in June 1971. RAIL PHOTOPRINTS

ABOVE: A view of the cramped internal arrangement, with its interlaced upper and lower compartments. COLOUR-RAIL

Project PEP

By the late-1960s, BR was working on a new generation of high-density electric multiple units for suburban and commuter lines. Many hundreds of first generation EMUs were built from the 1950s onwards based on the Mk 1 coach family, but were already regarded as old-fashioned by the 1960s.

The new high-density units would feature airy open saloons, wide, air-operated sliding doors for quick access/egress and gangways within the set, rather than the slam doors and separate compartments of older non-gangwayed stock, which was based on traditional steam era suburban carriage design.

Three experimental trains were built at York Works in 1971, two-car No. 2001 and four-car Nos. 4001/02, and

delivered to the Southern Region for testing. Under the SR classification system they became known as the 'PEP' units (Prototype Electro-Pneumatic), entering passenger service in June 1973.

Unlike earlier EMUs which generally had one or two motor cars per set, all axles of the 'PEP' trains were motored for rapid acceleration. The motor cars were originally allocated BR Class 461 with the non-driving cars Class 462, later becoming more conventionally numbered as Class 445 (4-PEP) and Class 446 (2-PEP).

Based on the SR Western Division at Wimbledon Park and Strawberry Hill for Waterloo suburban routes, they were extensively tested before entering passenger service, initially from Waterloo to Shepperton, Hampton Court and Chessington South. They were also tested on the South Eastern Division in August 1973, working from Cannon Street and Charing Cross to Bromley North, Dartford and Sevenoaks, although a series of failures saw them quickly despatched back to south-west London.

Nos. 4001/02 were painted in standard all-over BR blue, but No. 2001 was outshopped with an unpainted aluminium finish. They were intended to work as a 10-car set, but often worked individually.

Two-car No. 2001 was withdrawn from passenger service in August 1974, but the two four-car sets continued to work Waterloo suburban routes until May 1977. All three units then transferred to the departmental fleet.

An eleventh 'PEP' car, pantograph trailer ADB975431, was built and inserted into No. 2001 for 25kV AC testing on the Eastern and Scottish Regions. The three-car AC set became Class 920 in the departmental series and was the forerunner of the Class 313-315 EMUs of the late-1970s/early-1980s.

Nos. 4001/02 became SR departmental units Nos. 935056/057 with 056 eventually transferred to the Railway Technical Centre in Derby in June 1980 after several years in store. No. 057 was used to test several new bogie designs between 1979 and 1983 and also became part of the RTC fleet. However, all were out of use and stored by the mid-1980s; No. 056 was scrapped in 1986, followed by No. 920001 in 1987 and No. 057 in 1990.

The 'PEP' project greatly influenced BR's Second Generation EMUs from the late-1970s, especially the Class 313-315 dual-voltage/25kV AC sets and Southern Region Class 507/508s, most of which are still in service with various operators around the country. ●

ABOVE: A vision of the future at London Waterloo in 1973, as '4-PEP' No. 4001 waits for its next trip out to the suburbs of south-west London. A few years later Class 507 EMUs developed from the 'PEP' concept were introduced on these routes. COLOUR-RAIL

ABOVE: After its third-rail DC tests, '2-PEP' No. 2001 gained a third car and became a 25kV AC test train. On August 10, 1975 No. 920001 stands at Clacton. Note the unpainted aluminium bodyshell. COLOUR-RAIL

ABOVE: The North Eastern Railway's first electric locomotives were a pair of steeple-cab Bo-Bos built to work the steeply-graded Quayside Yard branch in Newcastle in 1902/03. In BR days, the pair show off their NER lined green livery at Heaton depot. COLOUR-RAIL

Electric Pioneers

Although electric trains were seen as a good solution for suburban railways in the early decades of the 20th century, railway companies were more reluctant to consider them for main lines until much later. However, a few British railway companies did investigate the potential of electric traction before the Second World War.

Electrification as a solution for busy main line railways took some years to gain traction in Britain, thanks to the ready supplies of good quality coal and, in some cases, conservative top-level management at the big railway companies. However, within the industry there were committed advocates of electric traction who recognised the efficiencies it could deliver on busy or steeply-graded lines.

The North Eastern Railway (NER) was one such advocate, developing a small series of prototype electric locomotives for different uses in the north-east of England. As one of the largest and most profitable railway companies in the country, with immense freight traffic from

the coal, steel and engineering industries of the north-east, the NER was in a good position to test the new form of traction.

Tyneside pioneers

As part of a 1902 scheme to electrify the North Tyneside suburban network, NER Chief Mechanical Engineer Wilson Worsdell proposed the electrification of a three-quarter mile, steeply-graded and horseshoe-shaped line between Trafalgar Yard and Quayside Yard in Newcastle. Passing through three single-line tunnels, the line had gradients as steep as 1-in-27 and sharp curves that presented a formidable challenge for steam traction.

Conditions inside the tunnels were appalling; steam locomotives had to work flat out to conquer the gradient, producing huge quantities of choking smoke that could not be dispersed from the tunnels. Electrification was the obvious answer.

Two steeple-cab locomotives were built to work the line in 1902/03, derived from a 1900 machine designed and built by General Electric and British Thomson-Houston for the Milano-Varese railway in Italy. ES1 and ES2 were built to draw current from both third rail and overhead supply as the Quayside branch featured the former in its tunnels and the latter elsewhere. BTH sub-contracted the supply of mechanical components to Brush

ABOVE: LNER No. 11 is one of the 'EF1' Bo-Bo freight locomotives built by the NER for the Newport-Shildon experimental electrification in 1914. On May 20, 1933 the locomotive was stored at Darlington Works after the end of electric operation. COLOUR-RAIL

Electrical Engineering in Loughborough.

The specification called for the locomotives to start a train of 150t on the steepest section, haul 300t at 14mph on level track and complete the journey from the quayside in four and a half minutes.

The electrified line was operational from June 5, 1905 and both locomotives performed exceptionally well. A few years later the bow collectors on the bonnets were replaced by a pantograph on the cab roof. The pair remained in operation until the line was de-electrified and they were replaced by diesel shunters in February 1964.

The locomotives were given the designation 'ES1' by the LNER in October 1945, and numbered as Nos. 1 and 2 until June 1946 when they became Nos. 6480/81. In April 1948, they gained their BR numbers 26500/501.

In 1968 No. 26500 was transferred to Leicester Railway Museum but was taken into the National Collection when that museum closed in 1977. It currently resides at Locomotion in Shildon, not far from its former Tyneside home.

Electric Expansion

The success of electric operation in Newcastle, even on a short branch, and developments elsewhere in Europe convinced Worsdell's successor, Sir Vincent Raven, of the advantages of main line electrification on a wider scale.

He gained authority from the NER to demonstrate his ideas on the busy 18-mile freight line from Shildon Yard to Newport Yard in Co. Durham. Shildon was a collecting point for coal from the surrounding coalfields, while Newport was a distribution hub for coal to docks, steel and iron works in the Stockton-on-Tees area. This traffic dated back to the original Stockton & Darlington Railway

ABOVE: Wills cigarette card of Sir Vincent Raven's impressive NER No. 13 – a unique express locomotive that never worked a revenue earning train. RAILWAY MAGAZINE ARCHIVE

of 1825 and remained hugely important and profitable for its successor, the NER.

Electrification began in 1914 using a 1,500V DC overhead system. The first stage opened on July 1, 1915, and the entire route was operational by January 10, 1916. The infrastructure was designed with simplicity and economy in mind.

Ten centre-cab Bo-Bo freight locomotives (Nos. 3-12) were built in 1914-19. Nine were ready by December 1914, but the tenth (No. 12) was not completed until December 1919, after the end of the First World War.

The locomotives were built at Darlington Works to Raven's design, featuring Siemens electrical equipment and four 275hp traction motors, giving a one-hour rating of 1,100hp. They were designed to haul a 1,400t train on the level at a minimum speed of 25mph. Loads were initially limited to 1,000t, increased to 1,400 tons (70 wagons) in November 1922. The locomotives

were well regarded by crews and were considered to be slightly superior to Raven's powerful 'Q6' 0-8-0 mineral engines.

Two pantographs were fitted on top of the cab roof with high-tension electrical equipment in the end compartments. Bufferbeams and drawgear were mounted directly on the bogies. They were based at Shildon shed's No. 3 roundhouse, which was converted to house all ten locomotives.

Unfortunately there was not enough traffic to keep all ten locomotives employed, due to restrictions on coal exports in 1914-18 but later because of the slump in trade in the 1920s and 1930s.

In July 1928, Nigel Gresley proposed the conversion of one locomotive into a 1,000hp diesel-electric for Peterborough-London coal traffic, retaining the bogies and motors, but with a new superstructure with end cabs. However, the rebuild never took place.

By the mid-1930s, much of the NER ▶

ABOVE: The success of the NER's 1,500V DC electrification led the LNER to pursue it for the busy trans-Pennine Woodhead route in the late-1930s, although work wasn't completed until 1954. 'EM1' Bo+Bo No. 26000 *Tommy* was the first of the Woodhead electric locomotives, completed to a Sir Nigel Gresley design in 1940. On September 19, 1964, the ex-LNER prototype backs into Sheffield Victoria observed by a gallery of enthusiasts. RAIL PHOTOPRINTS

overhead equipment was ready for replacement, but the falling traffic levels could not justify the expense and the LNER decided to revert to steam haulage. Shildon Yard closed in January 1935, and all ten electrics were stored at Darlington Works.

Around the same time, the LNER was investigating the electrification of the Manchester-Sheffield-Wath 'Woodhead' route (see below) at 1,500V DC and proposed the conversion of the 'EF1s' for banking duties. In 1941, No. 11 moved to Doncaster Works for modifications, including more powerful motors, increasing the one hour rating to 1,256hp, additional sandboxes and electric lights.

Acknowledging their new status, all ten locomotives were classified as 'EB1' (Electric Banking 1) by the LNER in October 1945, although only one had been rebuilt at that stage. In 1949, BR decided not to convert the remaining locomotives for banking duties, and they were redesignated as 'EF1s' (Electric Freight 1s). With no other work in prospect, they were withdrawn in August 1950 and scrapped soon afterwards.

However, 'EB1' No. 11, by now numbered No. 26510, was transferred to the new Ilford EMU depot in London in 1949 to act as depot pilot. It remained in service until November 1960, when the Liverpool Street-Shenfield line was converted from 1,500V DC to 25kV AC supply. BR did consider converting the locomotive, by now renumbered Departmental No. 100, to AC operation but the plan was dropped and it was finally withdrawn in April 1964.

Unlucky No. 13

After the initial success of the Shildon-Newport electrification, the NER developed ambitious plans to electrify its section of East Coast Main Line between York and Newcastle. Authorisation was granted in March 1920 to build a prototype electric passenger locomotive.

The impressive NER No. 13 had a 2-Co-2 wheel arrangement, with 6ft 8in diameter driving wheels, and was built at Darlington with Metropolitan-Vickers electrical equipment. Powered by six 300hp traction motors, it was designed to haul 14 bogie coaches (450t) at a minimum of 65mph on straight and level track and start the same load on a rising gradient of 1-in-78. Each driving axle was powered by two motors using geared quill drives.

These allowed the axles to move vertically in their hornguides without transmitting movement to the driving motors.

An electric boiler was fitted to provide steam heating for passenger coaches.

No. 13 was completed in May 1922 and in that summer it ran trials on the Shildon-Newport line. Unfortunately, in January 1923 the NER ceased to exist and the newly-formed LNER dropped the electrification scheme. No. 13 never worked again, but it did appear at the Stockton & Darlington Centenary celebration in July 1925, hauled by a 'J71' 0-6-0T.

Despite being unlikely to find any further work, No. 13 survived for many years, being stored with the redundant 'EF1/EB1' Bo-Bos at Darlington Works until 1947, and then moved to South Gosforth EMU depot on Tyneside. Renumbered No. 6999 in 1946 and classified 'EE1' by the LNER, it became No. 26600 under BR in 1948 but was finally withdrawn in August 1950. On December 15, 1950 it was dragged to a scrapyard near Rotherham and broken up. It is not known why the LNER was so reluctant to dispose of No. 13, despite the fact that it didn't work under its own power for almost 30 years after 1922. According to one contemporary source, when examined in January 1946, No. 13 had run just 2,200 miles.

Rock on *Tommy*

Despite abandoning the NER's planned electrification between York and Newcastle, and ending electric operation of the Shildon-Newport line in 1935, just a year later the LNER announced its intention to electrify the Manchester-Sheffield-Wath 'Woodhead' route.

Immensely busy with coal traffic from Yorkshire to Lancashire, and a wealth of other traffic in the opposite direction, this trans-Pennine route was notoriously congested and difficult to work with steam traction. The single bore Woodhead tunnels were unpleasant, if not downright dangerous, for loco crews who often had to lay on the footplate floor with rags over their faces to avoid choking on the ever-present fumes.

In November 1936, the LNER chose to modernise the route for 1,500V DC operation, which was already in use on the Manchester, South Junction & Altrincham (MSJ&A) suburban line. The programme included the construction of 69 mixed traffic ('EM1') Bo+Bos, nine 'EM2' express passenger and ten 'EB1' banking locomotives. Work started on the core 'EM1' design first and in January 1939, electrical equipment for 70 locomotives was ordered from Metropolitan Vickers in Manchester, with construction to take

place at the LNER's Doncaster Works. The scheme was halted by the outbreak of war in 1939 and the initial order was reduced to one prototype in November of that year.

Built to a design by Nigel Gresley, the 'EM1' had an unusual design with two four-wheel bogies linked by an intermediate coupling. The drawgear and buffers were mounted on the outer ends of the bogies, eliminating transmission of traction or braking forces through the locomotive body. The concept was based on a design supplied by Metropolitan Vickers to South African Railways.

The choice of a Bo+Bo wheel arrangement was primarily driven by LNER concerns over the capital cost of the project. It proved to be a mistake because of the excessive weight transfer when accelerating, causing a reduction in the load on the leading axle, wheelslip and a loss of adhesion. A heavier Co+Co design would have been better suited to braking heavy unfitted trains on the long descents found either side of Woodhead Tunnel.

Prototype No. 6701 was completed in August 1940. Initial dynamic trials involved towing it behind a steam locomotive between Doncaster and Retford. No. 6701 was officially added to stock in September 1941 and ran trials on the MSJ&A with loaded wagons or empty coaches. The 'EM1' was fitted with regenerative braking and this was tested by attaching two 'J39' 0-6-0s working flat-out in the opposite direction. No. 6701 returned to Doncaster

in October 1941, and was then stored awaiting the cessation of hostilities.

No. 6701 was renumbered No. 6000 in June 1946 and, to gain more extensive operating experience, was prepared for loan to Netherlands Railways (NS) in 1947. Its suspension gear was altered, maintained, and thoroughly cleaned; resulting in improved riding during further trials.

No. 6000 was shipped via the Harwich-Hook of Holland train ferry in September 1947, and was in traffic by the 15th of the month. Between September 1947 and March 1952 it covered around 310,000 miles on the Dutch network, working both passenger trains and freights weighing up to 1,750t.

On its return to 'Blighty', No. 6000 was officially named *Tommy* at London Liverpool Street on June 30, 1952 – an affectionate nickname coined by the Dutch, and also used for British troops who had only recently helped to liberate the country. No. 26000 remained on the Great Eastern until March 1953 when it was transferred to Gorton shed in Manchester ready to start work on the electrified MSW line.

Between October 1950 and August 1953, a further 57 production 'EM1s' were delivered by Gorton Works and worked the route until it was closed in July 1981. However, *Tommy* was withdrawn a decade earlier, shortly after passenger services between Sheffield Victoria and Manchester Piccadilly ceased. It was retired in March 1970 and, sadly, this significant locomotive was not rescued for preservation. ●

ABOVE: A classic period piece as an almost-new 'Deltic' passes NER electric No. 26500 at Manors, Newcastle-upon-Tyne. The electric is working from the third-rail supply installed by the NER on its Tyneside suburban system. I.S. CARR/RAILWAY MAGAZINE ARCHIVE

Bulleid-Raworth 'Booster' Electrics

The constituent railway companies that merged to form the Southern Railway were early converts to electric traction, especially for the heavy commuter traffic in and around London (see page 86). In the 1920s and 1930s, third-rail electrification was gradually extended away from the capital and its suburbs, reaching Brighton in 1933, Eastbourne and Hastings by May 1935, Waterloo-Portsmouth in 1937 and the Brighton-Worthing-Havant 'Coastway' line in 1938.

While a range of Electric Multiple Units (EMUs) was built to run local, semi-fast and express passenger services, the Southern Railway identified a need for a fleet of locomotives to handle goods and heavy passenger trains, such as Victoria-Newhaven Marine boat trains. However, one problem for comparatively short locomotives was that, unlike multi-car EMUs, they could become stranded at low speeds on gaps in third-rail, which were necessary at level crossings, junctions and other complex locations. This could also lead to 'snatching' as the locomotive comes on and off the power, risking the breakage of couplings.

A solution was devised by SR electrical engineer Alfred Raworth who, with O.V.S. Bulleid designed two prototype six-axle electric locomotives built at Ashford Works in 1940/41 and 1948. Raworth's design combined a motor-generator 'booster' set with a large flywheel on the shaft between the two, much like a modern model railway mechanism. Traction current fed a large motor which turned a drive shaft with the flywheel and fed into the generator. Generator output could be combined with third-rail power to reduce or boost the voltage applied to the traction motors. The flywheel ensured that the generator continued to turn when there was no contact with the third rail, ensuring an uninterrupted supply of power to the traction motors.

Two 'booster' sets were fitted, one for each bogie. It was not sufficient to allow the locomotives to work "off the juice" as the load on the generator while under power meant it would quickly consume the stored kinetic energy. They needed attentive driving, to ensure they were not brought to a halt on a gap and the booster set allowed to run down.

Raworth mitigated losses when changing from electrical to kinetic energy by providing 26 'taps' that altered resistances in the field coils of the generator, rather than large, heavily built resistances for the motors. These made the construction much lighter and easier to maintain. Instead of wastefully consuming power it didn't need, the controller simply altered how much power was generated.

Numbered CC1 and CC2 in Bulleid's French-inspired series, the locomotives were exempt from the wartime restrictions on new construction because of the potential labour and cost saving advantages they promised over steam traction. However, shortages of materials delayed their completion on several occasions. Taking advantage of existing jigs, the two locomotives shared their welded cab construction with the '2-HAL' EMUs, and the family resemblance was immediately obvious!

Internally, No. CC2 differed slightly from the first machine, but the real change came with the third locomotive, built by British Railways at Brighton

ABOVE: The third of the Bulleid Raworth electric locomotives, No. 20003, at London Victoria on May 15, 1949, less than a year after it was completed at Brighton Works. RAIL PHOTOPRINTS

ABOVE: Nos. 20003 and 20001 stabled at Brighton on September 1, 1968 showing the many detail differences between the Southern built locomotives of 1941 and their 1948-built sister. PATRICK KINGSTON/RAILWAY MAGAZINE ARCHIVE

Works in 1948. Numbered 20003 from new (CC1 and CC2 became Nos. 20001/002 under BR), it featured a modified design by SR electrical engineer S. B. Warder (later British Transport Commission Chief Electrical Engineer). No. 20003 differed externally from its earlier sisters, being 2in longer with flat 'Queen Mary' 4-SUB style cab ends and a simpler, cheaper to build design. However, it weighed 5t more than Nos. 20001/002 due to internal equipment changes.

Six traction motors provided a total of 1,470hp, allowing them to handle 1,000t goods and 750t passenger trains with ease. The trio became particularly associated with boat trains to Newhaven Marine, on which they replaced ex-LBSCR 'H1/H2' 4-4-2s in 1949. For safety reasons, tramway style DC catenary was installed in various SR yards rather than third-rail supply. To collect current from this, the 'booster' electrics were fitted with a diamond pattern cross-arm pantograph.

Powerful, reliable and efficient, they led an unremarkable life doing what they were built to do on the SR Central Section. However, no more third-rail electric locomotives were built until the 'HA' (Class 71s) of 1959, which

also employed the 'booster' concept, although were very different otherwise.

All three were withdrawn in the winter of 1968/1969 without receiving their allocated Class 70 TOPS computer numbers. No. 20003 was first to go, in

October 1968, followed by Nos. 20002 in December 1968 and 20001 in January 1969. None of this pioneering trio survived, although they can be regarded as a successful experiment in producing reliable 750V DC third-rail locomotives. ●

ABOVE: Heading what is likely to be a race day special to Tattenham Corner, No. 20001 passes Clapham Junction in 1952 with Pullman Cars in tow. By now the locomotive has been repainted in BR black with silver trim, in common with other early diesel and electric prototypes. RAIL PHOTOPRINTS

ABOVE: In later years, No. 87101 *Stephenson* was part of the Railfreight Distribution fleet and a regular fixture at depot open days. COLOUR-RAIL

Thyristor Testbed: 87101

For the extension of electric operation to Glasgow in 1974, BR ordered 36 5,000hp Bo-Bo locomotives. While 35 of the class were conventional machines developed from the earlier Class 86s, in particular the three Class 86/1 5,000hp rebuilds, the final locomotive was constructed by GEC/BR as a testbed for new thyristor traction control technology. Originally allocated No. 87036, it was actually numbered 87101 to prevent any confusion with the standard tap-changer control locomotives.

Completed in March 1975, No. 87101 spent many months on test before entering regular revenue-earning use in 1976. The locomotive could be operated in conventional or advanced mode for tests and underwent lengthy static and dynamic tests to assess the new technology. It was later named *Stephenson*, gaining 'plates transferred from No. 87001 when it became *Royal Scot*.

However, after its initial tests, No. 87101 settled into regular use alongside the other Class 87s, hauling West Coast Main Line passenger and freight services and eventually becoming part of the Railfreight fleet after sectorisation in the late-1980s. Unlike its Willesden based sisters, the prototype was normally based at Crewe Electric Depot. It remained as part of the Railfreight Distribution fleet until RfD was sold to Wisconsin Central in 1997, working its final years for English Welsh & Scottish Railway (EWS) on freight and charter trains before a major failure led to its withdrawal in 1999. It was sold to Alstom as a spare parts donor to keep the other '87s' going, stripped of all reusable components and eventually scrapped by Harry Needle Railroad Co. at Barrow Hill in February 2002.

Development work undertaken with No. 87101 directly influenced the later Class 87/2 project of the mid-1980s and led to the introduction of the Class 90s (originally designated as '87/2s') from 1987. ●

Breaking the Mould: 89001

ABOVE: Much of No. 89001's early testing took place on the West Coast Main Line with the BREL 'International Train', which was built to attract export orders and eventually sold to Irish Rail. In May 1987, an interesting ensemble arrives at Crewe led by the 'Badger'. It includes RTC test cars *Prometheus* and Test Car 10, followed by the International Train.
COLOUR-RAIL

From the late-1950s until the Class 87s of 1972-75, all production BR electric locomotives followed a similar pattern of construction. It wasn't until 1983 that a very different 25kV AC electric prototype was ordered from BREL/Brush Traction as the forerunner of a proposed new class of powerful 125mph Co-Co machines.

Built very slowly at BREL Crewe Works in 1984-87, No. 89001 bore some resemblance to the prototype HST power cars, but was a 5,850hp six-axle locomotive incorporating many advanced electrical features. It was intended for 125mph operation on the East Coast Main Line, which was being electrified in stages between Huntingdon and Edinburgh at the time. Although this order eventually went to GEC Traction's lighter, more powerful Class 91, the '89' went on to play a major role in the development of electric locomotives for the Channel Tunnel.

Eventually completed in 1987, the locomotive moved to Brush Traction in Loughborough and then the RTC in Derby for extensive static and electrical tests, as well as structural and type test approval before it could venture out on the main line. Test runs were also made at the Old Dalby test centre in mid-1987, albeit propelled by a diesel as the line was not electrified at the time.

After acceptance by BR, it was unleashed on the West Coast Main Line. By October 1987 it had run more than 10,000 miles and proved to be highly satisfactory on test runs from Crewe over the northern section of the WCML, including the challenging climb to Shap. Gauging issues precluded it from working into London Euston, which meant it could not be used on WCML InterCity services, but at the end of 1987 it was switched to the East Coast Main Line, based at Hornsey.

Nicknamed the 'Badger', No. 89001 worked alongside the East Coast Class 91 fleet as it grew, and as electrification was gradually extended north in 1988-90, the locomotives were able to reach Peterborough, Leeds and York on test trains, charters and scheduled trains. Regular duties included peak hour Peterborough-King's Cross commuter trains in 1988.

In May/June 1988, the locomotive visited the IVA international transport exhibition in Hamburg, along with a Class 90, Class 91 and a 'Sprinter' DMU, travelling via the Harwich-Hook of Holland train ferry and by rail through the Netherlands and Germany.

Passenger and test use continued until a serious failure in July 1992, after which it was withdrawn by BR and sold to a group of Brush Traction employees based at the Midland Railway Centre in Derbyshire. However, that was not the end of the story; in 1996 No. 89001 was bought by Sea Containers Ltd, owners of the GNER franchise operating ECML services, and returned to working order in 1997. It worked alongside Class 91s on the King's Cross-Leeds/Bradford route, smartly turned out in GNER dark blue until another major failure in late-1999 sidelined it for several months. It returned in 2000 but suffered the same fate as many advanced prototypes, its availability reduced by lengthy depot visits waiting for bespoke replacement components. In 2001 it was withdrawn by GNER and retired from main line duty for the second time. It is now owned by the AC Locomotive Group and based at Barrow Hill, where repairs are being undertaken to return it to working order. Another return to main line operation has been suggested for some time, and may well allow this powerful, charismatic machine to show off its capabilities in front line service again. We await further developments with interest! ●

ABOVE: On September 9, 1997, No. 89001 stands at London King's Cross alongside GNER's No. 91027 and two more '91s' as they prepare for their next northbound dash over the East Coast Main Line. RAILWAY MAGAZINE ARCHIVE

Hover & Fly

For decades, engineers have tried to break away from conventional rails and tracks to create faster, more efficient trains that use air currents or magnets to float smoothly and quickly along guided tracks.

ABOVE: The largest of the Aérotrain prototypes – I80-250, before it was rebuilt for 350kph operation. PHILIPPE CHATRIOT ARCHIVE ASSOCIATION DES AMIS DE JEAN BERTIN

Very much part of the 'White Heat of Technology' prevalent in Britain in the 1960s, Tracked Hovercraft was an experimental high-speed train combining two great British inventions, the hovercraft and the linear induction motor. The idea was to produce a train that could deliver 250mph inter-city services with lower capital costs than conventional high-speed railways. In concept, it was similar to the French Aérotrain (see above) and other hovertrain experiments of the 1960s, and it suffered a similar fate when funding was cut and it was cancelled in 1973.

Having developed the technology using scale models, the Tracked Hovercraft team spent several years persuading the UK Government to fund a full-size test track and train.

In the early-1970s, an elevated test track was eventually built between Earith and Denver Sluice in the Cambridgeshire/Norfolk Fens. Standing around 6ft clear of the ground, the four-mile track was the first section of a proposed 20-mile test track where trains would be expected to reach 300mph.

On February 7, 1973, the full-size vehicle – Research Test Vehicle 31 (RTV31) managed a maximum of 104mph over a one-mile section section. Even then though, there were strong rumours that the project was facing imminent cancellation.

Unfortunately, even before the test track was operational, British Rail was making good progress with its Advanced Passenger Train (APT) and Government advisors favoured it over the untested new technology, especially as entirely new infrastructure would be required for a passenger-carrying TH network.

Opponents of TH also pointed to the rapid development and superiority of rival MAGLEV technology.

Just a week after the February 1973 test run, funding for the Tracked Hovercraft project was cancelled and attention turned to developing a commercially viable MAGLEV system.

The Fenland test track was dismantled, but RTV31 survived for many years at Cranfield University and is now on display at the Railworld centre in Peterborough.

ABOVE: All that survives of the cancelled Tracked Hovercraft project is a section of concrete track and the RTV31 test vehicle, both preserved at Railworld in Peterborough. WIKIMEDIA COMMONS

French Rival

In parallel with the British Tracked Hovercraft scheme, French engineer Jean Bertin was developing a similar vehicle known as Aérotrain.

Between 1965 and 1977, he worked on several increasingly large prototype vehicles that used an air cushion and jet engines to suspend the train above the track. Aérotrain could, in theory, travel at very high speeds without the technical complexity and expensive tracks of magnetic levitation.

The first 6.7km long test track was built in February 1966 for Aérotrains 01 and 02, using an abandoned railway formation. A second track built from aluminium and asphalt was built parallel to the first track in 1969 for Aérotrain prototype S44.

In 1969, a third, 18km test track was built to test the large Aérotrain prototype I80. This more extensive elevated track, designed for 400kph operation, was built alongside the SNCF main line between Saran and Ruan, north of Orleans and was envisaged as the first section of a future Paris-Orleans line. A platform at each end of the line allowed the train to be turned.

Five prototypes were built; Aérotrain 01 was a half-scale model propelled by a three-bladed reversible-pitch propeller and later Turbomeca jet engine. Aérotrain 02 was another scale prototype powered by a Pratt & Whitney turbojet engine.

However, Aérotrain S44 was a full-size passenger-carrying car intended for short-distance service at speeds of up to 200kph, such as airport links. It was equipped with a Linear Induction Motor propulsion system. Finally, Aérotrain I-80 was a full-size passenger-carrying car for inter-city service. It was 25.6m long, had 80 seats and was propelled by two Turbomeca 1,600hp turboshaft

ABOVE: A 1960s vision of a high speed future: Aérotrain I80 on the concrete test track north of Orleans. WIKIMEDIA COMMONS

engines powering a ducted propeller.

I-80 was later rebuilt for 350kph and re-designated as the I-80 Haute Vitesse (high speed). It set a world speed record of 417.6kph on March 5, 1974 with a peak speed of 430.4kph.

In 1970, Rohr Industries in the USA decided to develop a tracked air-cushion vehicle as part of a project to sponsor development of new mass-transit technology to meet future transit requirements.

The Rohr prototype, officially named the Urban Tracked Air Cushion Vehicle (UTACV) but better known as the Rohr Aerotrain, was propelled by linear motor and was designed to carry 60 passengers at 150mph (240kph).

However, the project was mothballed in 1975, and the French project was abandoned in 1977 due to lack of funding, the death of Jean Bertin, and the advent of SNCF's *Train a Grand Vitesse* (TGV)

as the French Government's preferred high-speed transport solution.

MAGLEV

Derived from magnetic levitation, MAGLEV is a system that uses magnets to move vehicles without making contact with the ground. Vehicles travel along a guideway using magnets to create both lift and propulsion, reducing friction to a great extent and, potentially, allowing very high speeds.

Compared to conventional wheeled trains, there is much less wear and tear to vehicles and track but MAGLEV systems have proved to be much more expensive to construct.

The principle was first discovered in the 1900s but it wasn't until the late-1940s that British electrical engineer Eric Laithwaite developed the first working model of a linear induction motor.

ABOVE: The USA's jet-powered LIMTV on test at Pueblo, Colorado. BRUCE MCALLISTER. U.S. NATIONAL ARCHIVES PUBLIC DOMAIN

ABOVE: British Rail's low-speed MAGLEV prototype on the test track with the Railway Technical Centre in Derby. RAILWAY MAGAZINE ARCHIVE

Linear motors do not require physical contact between the vehicle and guideway and became a common fixture of advanced transportation systems in the 1960s and 1970s.

British Rail's Railway Technical Centre at Derby (RTC) was an early pioneer in the MAGLEV field, building a working prototype and track through the RTC in the 1970s. However, the world's first commercial MAGLEV people mover officially opened between Birmingham International and Birmingham Airport in 1984.

Operating over a 600m elevated track at up to 26mph, it closed in 1995 due to reliability problems and was replaced by a cable-operated people mover.

Despite decades of research and development, MAGLEV lines are in operation in just three countries – Japan, South Korea and China.

Germany was, for many years, a leader in MAGLEV technology, opening its first Transrapid demonstration track at the IVA International Transport Exhibition in 1979. The 1.6km M-Bahn line in West Berlin ran between 1989 and 1991 and was the second commercial application of the technology.

On a much larger scale, Transrapid built a 19.6-mile test track in the Emsland region with turning loops at each end. Prototype trains regularly ran at up to 420kph (260mph) and paying passengers were carried as part of the testing process. Construction took place between 1980 and 1984 and development continued well into the 2000s, leading to the sale of the technology to China for its Shanghai Airport shuttle. Shanghai's £900m Transrapid line began operations in 2004, running at a maximum commercial speed of 431kph (268mph). Trains built by Siemens and ThyssenKrupp cover the 30km (18 mile) route in just seven minutes and 20 seconds. On test, one of the vehicles attained a maximum of 501kph (311mph).

Various Transrapid lines were also proposed in Germany, including Hamburg-Berlin and Munich city centre to Munich Airport lines. Unfortunately, a serious collision with a maintenance vehicle on the Emsland line in 2006 killed 23 people and no further passengers were carried. At the end of 2011 Transrapid's licence expired and was not renewed, and in early-2012 permission was given to demolish the Transrapid elevated track, depot and facilities.

Japan pushes ahead

Japan has a relatively low-speed line in Osaka, but also has JR Central's world record-breaking L0 test line, which has run at over 600kph (375mph) on test. Opened in 2013, the test line has provided valuable experience for the planned Tokyo-Nagoya-Osaka Chuo Shinkansen MAGLEV line, which is expected to be completed in two stages, to Nagoya by 2027 and Osaka by 2045.

Expected to cost around £57 billion,

ABOVE: The world's first public MAGLEV line ran from Birmingham International BR station to the nearby airport terminal from 1984 until it was replaced by cable-worked cars in 1995. MALTA GC/WIKIPEDIA

ABOVE: Germany spent many years developing its Transrapid MAGLEV system at the Emsland test track, but the only commercial application was a short line to Shanghai Airport built largely as a sales tool for the technology. The test track closed after a fatal collision in 2006. WIKIMEDIA COMMONS

85% of the route will be in tunnel and trains running at 505kph (314mph) will complete the journey from Tokyo to Osaka in just 67 minutes.

Other commercial MAGLEV lines around the world include the Incheon Airport line in South Korea, which opened in 2016.

It is 6.1km long with six stations and a 110kph (68mph) operating speed.

Two extensions of 9.7km (six miles) and 37.4km (23.2 miles) are planned and once completed it will become a circular line.

While MAGLEV lines have been proposed over many years in the USA, Italy, the UK, Germany, Australia, Switzerland, India, Iran, Taiwan and Hong Kong, very few schemes have ever come to fruition, largely thanks to high construction costs,

lack of connectivity with existing rail networks, inflexibility and, in Europe, opposition to intrusive elevated tracks marching across the landscape. However, with Japan and China both pursuing long-distance schemes linking major cities over the next 30 years, MAGLEV could yet deliver on the promises made by its proponents since the 1960s. ●

ABOVE: The Shanghai Airport Transrapid operates at speeds of up to 268mph and covers the 18-mile route in just seven minutes and 20 seconds. WIKIMEDIA COMMONS